aftermath:

A GRANDDAUGHTER'S STORY OF LEGACY, HEALING & HOPE

By Allison Nazarian

ACCLAIM

When you see someone every day, you think you know them, but Allison's powerful story shows you that all is not what it seems to the outside world. Allison takes the very courageous step of tearing down the curtain on her life and shows us what it was like to grow up as a "3G," and the daughter of a depressed mother and the granddaughter of a woman who had to tell the story of her survival. The burden of the story had very different effects on the three powerful women in this book, and it drove the trajectory of each of their lives in a different way. I commend Allison for being brave enough to share a very private story and for coming out stronger on the other side.

~ Mariana H.

Please don't take this the wrong way, but what I did not want to read is another book about the Holocaust. I thought I had read all of the possible kinds of stories related to that horrible period in history, and yet I was wrong. Allison, this book is so different, so sobering, so nuanced in its telling of a truly unique and, at the same time, beautiful and sad story. I know it wasn't easy for you to share it, but in doing so, you have shared so much light with the rest of us. Thank you from the bottom of my heart for this story.

~ J.R.

It seems more difficult these days to find a book that goes beyond skimming the surface, yet avoids unnecessary drama. *Aftermath* is that rare gem of a book that goes deep, and its author blesses the reader with her thoughtfulness and self-reflection. *Aftermath* is about more than the Holocaust: it's about our interconnectedness as families and human beings, and the grace that comes from the recognition of those connections.

~ Reese Spykerman

You're brave and your story is incredible. I mean that, and I am not someone who would usually say things like that. I was moved by your honesty and your story of hope and healing that really does reflect its title. I admire and salute your honesty and your self-awareness. You are a gift, as is this book.

~ D.I.

[This book is] thoughtful, well written, descriptive, raw and honest. I would highly recommend it to others to share in the sensitivity of the Holocaust as a subject, as a character and a part of who you are as well as the rest of generations to come. Your lessons learned are admirable, thought-provoking, harsh and inspirational.

~ Wendy Wiseberg

Also by Allison Nazarian

Love Your Mess

*Copywriting 101 for Small Businesses,
Entrepreneurs, Coaches & Consultants*

The One-Minute Copywriter

aftermath:

A GRANDDAUGHTER'S STORY OF LEGACY, HEALING & HOPE

Allison Nazarian

ALLIE GIRL PUBLISHING

THE FAMILY

My maternal grandparents, Shlomo Reich and Pola Garfinkel (later, Sol and Paula Dash in America, and "Zeidy" and "Bubby" to me and many others), were born and raised in Poland, both members of large, traditional Jewish families. Both families were caught up by the happenings of history and became part of what later was called the Holocaust.

I know far more details surrounding my grandmother's story (for reasons that will be covered later) than I do about my grandfather's. Bubby was incarcerated in the Lodz Ghetto for about four years. While there, she watched her father, Aaron, die before her eyes. My grandmother, her surviving brother, Henry, and their mother, Leah, were taken in 1944 by train (or a "kettle car," as Bubby said with her accent) to the infamous Auschwitz. Upon arrival, Leah, my great-grandmother, was sent directly to the gas chambers, to her death.

Bubby was later "saved" from Auschwitz and sent off to various labor camps in and around Bremen, Germany, where she and other relatively strong young women were forced to perform hard labor, mostly related to clearing debris created as a result of the Allied bombings. In 1945, she was transferred to Bergen-Belsen, where she expected to be put to death. She was liberated from Bergen-Belsen in April of 1945.

My grandfather was in the camp known as Dachau. Unlike my grandmother, he had a number tattooed on his arm. That same number was immortalized on his gravestone. After the war, he and my grandmother met in a train station in Hanover, Germany. Both were refugees and had survived enormous trauma. They married in October of 1945. My mother, Lily (named after Leah), was born on January 12, 1947, in what had become a DP (Displaced Persons) camp in Bergen-Belsen.

In 1951, my grandparents and their only child, my mother, moved to Baltimore, Maryland, USA. Zeidy and Bubby died in 1991 and 2007, respectively. I came along in 1971 and my sister, Erica, in 1977. My mother died at the age of fifty-one in 1998, by suicide, four months after her first grandchild was born.

FAMILY TREE

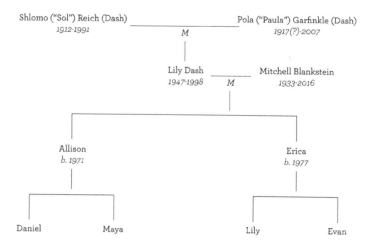

Shlomo ("Sol") Reich (Dash)
1912-1991

Pola ("Paula") Garfinkle (Dash)
1917(?)-2007

M

Lily Dash
1947-1998

Mitchell Blankstein
1933-2016

M

Allison
b. 1971

Erica
b. 1977

Daniel   Maya

Lily   Evan

AUTHOR'S NOTE

Welcome to my story.

While it has elements of history you may have experienced, learned something about, earned a PhD on, read about, heard about or saw a great movie about, this story is not the story of the Holocaust or the story of all Holocaust survivors and their families. In other words, there are elements of it that may seem different or unfamiliar or incongruent to you. That's OK.

While this book is a work of nonfiction, it is in no way objective or detached. You will also notice throughout that I use first-person excerpts in which my grandmother is the speaker, describing her various experiences. These "blurbs" come directly from transcripts of her many interviews, presentations and speeches over the years. They have not been edited.

To maintain anonymity in several instances, I have changed the names of individuals and/or identifying details such as physical properties, occupations and geographical locations. I have tried to recreate events, locales and conversations from my memories of them, as well as from journals, letters, interviews, source research and the memories of others. If in any case I have done so in a factually incorrect manner, this error is mine and mine alone.

EPIGRAPH

If you look deeply into the palm of your hand, you will see
your parents and all generations of your ancestors. All of
them are alive in this moment. Each is present in your body.
You are the continuation of each of these people.
~ Thich Nhat Hanh

I am the accumulation of the dreams of generations.
And their stories live in me like holy water.
~ Jewel

DEDICATION

For Bubby, the first and greatest light of my life.

For Zeidy, sweetness and loyalty personified.

For Mom, a beautiful and rare soul.

For Erica, who was there and who knows.

For Lily and Evan, so you will know someday.

For Daniel and Maya,
my greatest teachers and my reasons why.

INTRODUCTION

This is not your usual Holocaust book.

This is not even a Holocaust book; but without the Holocaust, it does not exist.

I gave birth to actual human beings twice in my life, and neither go-around compares to the gestation period of this book. Not even close. I'm certain, to the core of my soul, that this book needing to be born has affected my mental, emotional and physical state in all sorts of ways for several decades.

I don't think I have told this story perfectly. But now I have told it. I'm sure I have missed key points, but most of it is here. I also know that if I didn't get all of it out there and be done with being "in the process" of writing a book, that I may very well burst, all of my story going into bits with the rest of me.

The idea for this book was born in 1994, when I quit my shiny-new Manhattan ad agency job to travel to Eastern Europe with my mom and my grandmother. It first lived in a cute, little journal a good friend gifted me prior to the trip. (Thanks, Stu. I told you I'd give you props here!) It then went into hibernation until 1997 when I was a student at Columbia University's Graduate School of Journalism. I'd heard about the semi-famous "Sam Freedman Book Seminar," and I wanted in. After some vigorous back-and-forth with Professor Freedman on why this book carried with it a compelling enough idea to at least get me into this seminar, he opened the gates and I was in.

To give you an idea of time frame, I conceived my son, Daniel, about halfway into this same Spring 1997 semester. This same embryo is now a college student. Needless to say, it's been quite a gestation period for this book you hold in your hand—or on your smart device.

Part of the struggle and subsequent delay for me has always been, *Who am I writing this for? Is it for me? For my kids, both of whom are now on the cusp of adulthood? For my family? For my grandparents no longer with us? For the public? For academics? For the agent I once had? For the editors and publishing companies that are more discerning than ever? For the other "3Gs" and their families?* (3G, standing for "third generation," is a term I use to discuss the grandchildren of Holocaust survivors as a group.)

Every time I thought I knew who this was for and by extension, how it needed to be written, I was off. If I had a dollar for every proposal I wrote and revised, for every phone interview I painstakingly scheduled and recorded, for every iteration of title, website and approach or for every time I thought, *This is it; I'm on my way!*…well, let's just say, I'd have a nice collection of dollars.

It's hard to describe the emotions—and pressure—I have felt around this ongoing "thing." On one hand, I have always realized that this story is part of my purpose here on this planet. Not in some arrogant or self-important way, but in that quiet, knowing way of, *I cannot be who I need to be, fully, until this is outside of me and on paper.*

And yet, at some point, though, all of it had become enough. It had become too much. There was nothing pleasurable or freeing about this book for me—it was all burden. So I gave myself permission to put it aside and to give it a TBD (To Be Determined) status. I parted ways with the New York City agent who had agreed to represent me and sent him my thanks for his efforts. I tried not to beat myself up about what I viewed as a failure and worked to keep moving forward—after all, I was (am) a busy, self-employed mom with a business to run and two teenagers to raise. In other words, I had things to do.

Fast-forward to the end of 2015, when I began to be able to tolerate thinking about this book again. *What if,* I asked myself, *you wrote it to be finished, to put it out in the world? What if you stopped trying to get it perfect and, instead, got it done? What if,* I reasoned, using my own perfectionist-in-recovery lingo to debate the voice inside my head, *you proved the "done is the enemy of perfect" rule yet again?*

And there you are. The book you now read is all of that and maybe a bit more. It's in my voice, with my nuances, my stuff, my language and my perspective.

And although this book is for me, it's also for my family, my fellow 3Gs, their parents (the 2Gs) and the grandparents, of course.

It's also for anyone who cares about a good family story of heartbreak and trauma mixed in with genuine love.

Aftermath

It's for anyone who subscribes to the law of "Time + Tragedy = Humor."

It's about breaking old patterns and finding true healing, as painful and difficult as that is for anyone, no matter how strong or supported they may be.

It's about being OK with putting something imperfect out into the world. (That one makes me nervous, folks.)

It's about making mistakes that somewhere along the way you were taught you couldn't make.

It's about loving the people who raised you despite—or maybe because of—their shortcomings and limitations.

It's about forgiving them—and yourself—for all of that and so much more.

It's about reminding myself—and you—that it is never too late for whatever it is you feel called to do, complete or share.

This book is not perfect, nor am I. But it is perfectly done, and that is what matters now.

Thank you for being part of this journey.

Chapter 1

BUTTERFLIES

The dream started when I was around eight, sometime after we moved from a nice house in the suburbs to a nicer house in the suburbs. In it, I am in my then-new childhood home, running around aimlessly, chaotically. My family and I are in a frenzy, with only a few minutes to pack up our most important things. We can take only what we can carry on our backs, and we will likely not ever return to the home. In the dream, there is never enough time. There is never enough room for packing. I don't know what to take and what to leave behind. What do I need? What can I fit? Every cell in my body feels panicked, doomed. I am all at once paralyzed, terrified, running in circles.

I call it my "Holocaust Dream."

As all dreams—even nightmares—eventually end, so does this one. But the feelings of chaos and uncertainty don't. I've always lived with that feeling of being in a race against time, that feeling that I have to finish and to beat the clock or face some disaster. My intellectual brain knows that I am stronger than the dream, that no one is coming to "get" me. I remind myself that the panic about something that happened over seven decades ago— long before I was born—should not affect me. But it does. It has.

When my grandmother—Bubby —was growing up in Poland, she was an avid butterfly collector. She created display boxes with colorful, carefully pinned butterflies inside. She was meticulous and appreciated beautiful things. The collection was her pride and joy.

When the Germans came, she told me, she and her family had only a few minutes to pack their most important possessions into whatever they could carry on their own backs. She would have to leave her beloved butterflies behind. She was no longer a child, but this was something dear to her. She didn't know where she was headed, but surely there would be no room for something as beautiful, delicate and nonessential as a butterfly display.

Bubby never told me how she felt about leaving the collection behind, but I knew. The longing was in her voice and her demeanor; it was part of the story—heck, it *was* the story—but it wasn't actually shared in words. Instead, it lingered below, an ever-present reminder of how life could change in an instant, of how beauty and happiness could at the very same time be simple to attain and easy to lose. The loss of control, the loss of what was beautiful, the loss of life as it had been and would never be again—all of this had crushed her then, and it lived within her now.

I never saw her butterfly collection. But I knew what it

looked like. I knew. The fragile wings, the vibrant yellows and reds, the delicately placed pins, the rows. This was the first story I knew. It taught me that there is potential danger, heartache and suffering in every person and every situation, no matter how happy or contented they may feel in the moment. It taught me the impermanence of beauty. It also made me question effort and energy and time: Why invest in them if nothing lasts, if nothing is forever, if it can all be taken away? It taught me that getting attached to anything precious—even people—was dangerous. I knew I needed to be on top of everything, to control everything.

Above all, the butterflies represented fear. Fear, because I wondered, especially as a child, if such things could happen to me, too. If someone might someday come for me or for my family.

It filled me with fear, with the certainty that not only were horrible things horrible, but that wonderful things could turn horrible in an instant.

Bubby's stories always included wistful and loving descriptions of what life was like before—of the happiness and pleasure she had from her family, her friends, her schools and her wonderful life as a Jewish person in Lodz, the second-largest city in Poland. It sounded as if her life before the Nazi occupation had been at least as settled and stable—perhaps more so—than mine. So it stood to reason (at least in my young mind) that horror was not far removed from any of it.

Not all the lessons of the butterfly story were dark. I knew from my grandmother's example that triumph could come after tragedy. That you could lose everything, but you could get everything back, too. That the ugly didn't have to last forever, if you were strong and persistent, and lucky, too. That you could go through the worst thing possible and still come out a loving and loved person. That you could have a butterfly collection again.

Still, decades later, after Bubby had survived starvation, death camps and all the horrors of the Holocaust; after she'd raised a daughter, after her first granddaughter was born, she remembered the day she had to leave her butterflies as if it had happened the week before. I carried the story of the butterflies around with me like a secret. The panic, the impermanence, the uncertainty, the importance of the story being retold and remembered. If I didn't understand and carry it with me, who would?

Somewhere along the way, I thought I figured out how I could keep safe, untouched. If I did everything right, bad things would never happen to me. If I were the best, the first, the most, the prettiest, the smartest, then I would never be left behind or singled out. No one would take me away, so to speak, if they knew how special I was. I wouldn't be caught in an awful situation like Bubby and her butterflies if I stayed in control, if I were on top of everything, if I were the best.

CHAPTER 2

IN THE BEGINNING

In my family, the Holocaust was this thing. *Our* thing.
Like most anything else that is a part of who you are
and how you've grown up, it seemed, at the time, as normal
and natural as anything else in life. It was my Bubby and
Zeidy whose story informed and was incorporated into every aspect of my life. It was their tragedy, their heroism and
their history that everyone wanted to know about. It was
their story, and my grandmother's in particular as time went
on, that was center stage within our family and also within
the communities of which we were a part. It was this story
that created my mom, that had my mom believe she had to
marry my dad, that brought me into the world. I knew it so
well and yet, even now, I can't imagine what it was like: The
ghetto. Auschwitz. The gas chamber. The branded number
on my grandfather's arm. The watery soup. The stolen potatoes. The wiped-out family. My grandparents as new immi-

grants to the United States with next to nothing—no family, no material possessions, no English.

Everyone in my world knew that both of my maternal grandparents were survivors. They weren't the typical American grandma or grandpa who played golf or ate bacon. They weren't even the typical American-Jewish grandma or grandpa who, in my experience up until that point, all seemed to speak with New York accents and appeared sporadically in their grandkids' lives. Paula and Sol Dash, known in Poland as Pola and Shlomo, spoke with somewhat-stereotypical Yiddish accents and had never tried bacon (or golf) in their lives. They watched *60 Minutes* and read *The Washington Post* religiously, and they discussed everything that was important in their first language of Yiddish.

Paula—Bubby—was my primary caregiver in my earliest years. She lived with her husband, Sol, my Zeidy, in a two-bedroom apartment in Silver Spring, Maryland. Most of my earliest memories take place in that first apartment, the happy place of my childhood. It was a warm and cozy combination of chicken soup, cinnamon and frying oil. These two, my grandparents, were at the center of a very small core family that consisted of them, my mother, my father, myself and later, my sister, Erica.

My mom, Lily, was their only child. She'd been born in Bergen-Belsen, perhaps best known as the death camp where Anne Frank and her family were sent once they were discovered. After the war, places like Bergen-Belsen became Displaced Persons or "DP" camps, and that's where my mom was born in 1947, two years after what Bubby referred to as "TheLiberation" (all one word like that) and to everyone else was more simply "the end of the war."

Zeidy was a loyal sidekick to his wife. He did what he was told, spoke when given permission and deferred to the women around him. He was a short man with diabetes, and he was always overweight in a roly-poly, almost jolly, sort of way. I remember many times seeing him or hearing of him poking around in the refrigerator late at night, hoping to sneak out some contraband food when no one (specifically Bubby) was around. In his older years, he worked as a stock boy for Rodman's, a local Washington, DC-area drugstore chain. Truth be told, he didn't make much of himself professionally. His English was never very good, and his accent was strong. None of this seemed to matter much to him or others, though, and he was the most dear, sweet man who could converse with anyone, anywhere.

I cannot tell you how many men and women from the DC-area suburbs we lived in remember, to this day, talking with Sol Dash by the vending machines at the JCC (Jewish Community Center) in Rockville, Maryland, where Bubby would send him to exercise in the pool. However, Zeidy didn't like to exercise. Instead, he would go to the JCC as expected, water down his swimming trunks in the men's restroom and spend the entirety of his time there sitting in the vending machine room, enjoying snacks and figuring out which young boys and girls (and later young men and women) went to the Charles E. Smith Jewish Day School across the street and of those, who knew my sister, Erica, or me. Once he'd determined who knew us (and if they didn't, who *should* know us), he would share all sorts of detailed stories about his family history and his experience as a Holocaust survivor. While this may sound as if it were a strange or inappropriate topic of discussion, his delivery and his overall energy were so endearing and so tender that he, without exception, made friends and fans for life every time he started up a new conversation. And of course, after enough time had passed, Zeidy—now happily satiated with snacks and with his wet bathing suit in a bag—would return home to Bubby, who for many years had no reason to believe that he wasn't logging in lots of swimming hours.

It's possible that he could have shined brighter if he'd not been in the shadow of his articulate, go-getter wife for all of those years. The person who took center stage was Bubby. She ran the show. She was the one whose English was strong, whose accent was somehow impressive and not detrimental. She was the one who told me—and later everyone, everywhere—the stories. She was the one who remembered every last detail of every last story. No one questioned her version of the story. She was the one who could bring tears to your eyes even if you thought you'd heard it all. My grandmother managed to wear her tragedy in the most graceful way, sharing and re-sharing it through her speeches while still being one of the strongest and most optimistic people I have ever known. The Holocaust was my Bubby's badge of honor. She wore it proudly and she wore it well.

Zeidy died in 1991 when I was twenty and in college, and while he was around for most moments of those first twenty years, I knew and still know so little about him. By the mid-1980s, his mental and physical health had declined. Sadly, one of my most lasting memories of my Zeidy was of him walking up to complete strangers any time we were out and telling them in his Polish accent, *"I ate the grass. In Dachau, I ate the grass."* People would nod with concerned looks, but no one understood what he was talking about. It was undoubtedly the truth that he ate the grass, but I'd never known much of his story, so there wasn't much context to put it into. Most of his stories died with him and likely years before his physical body died. For that, I will always feel sadness and regret.

Yet, as Zeidy began to wane in his later years, Bubby began to expand and bloom. She continued on this path for most of the sixteen years that she lived on after his death. She was someone who began coming into her own during the time of life when most people wind down. She was truly adept at sharing her story of tragedy and using it to empower and inspire. She'd receive letters from men, women and children from all over the United States, explaining how deeply her story had touched them, how it had changed their lives, how they would never forget her. She spoke at Rotary clubs, churches, community colleges, universities and even the White House. In 1992, she took the train up to Philadelphia to speak to my Literature of the Holocaust class at the University of Pennsylvania. She did not seek out these engagements and these groups—they found her.

And then there was my mom. I had always known how enormously conflicted she was about her family history and about how it had affected her, yet I had no power to help or do a thing about it. I believe much of my hyperdeveloped sense of needing to control and to fix things for others (even when they have not indicated that they want my help or involvement) had its roots in growing up with a mother who believed that she had been born into a pretty damaged family, a less-than-ideal situation with two less-than-perfect parents. She was angry at the past she'd inherited. As a child, she'd longed to be a more "normal" American girl, with American parents with no accents and no history from a far-off and tragic place. She'd longed for grandparents and aunts and uncles. For brothers and sisters, for that matter. I had all of that and felt guilt because she didn't (and she never hesitated to tell me that she didn't). My mother always seemed angry over what her parents had been through—mad at her parents (as if they'd had a choice or an alternative), mad at God and maybe even mad at me for having such a close and loving relationship with my grandmother, and for being born into a vastly different situation. The regret and the resentment simmered inside of her for her entire life, until she took that life herself at the age of fifty-one.

Outwardly, Mom, in many ways, embraced her history and her parents' past. She studied the Holocaust academically on the graduate level and in her forties became a high school Jewish History teacher. She passionately engaged anyone who would listen in discussions, from a very academic and black-and-white perspective, about the Holocaust, while her mother wowed audiences with her emotional story that was anything but academic or black and white. On many occasions, she challenged her mother, Bubby, about a name of a specific camp or the year in which a specific event took place. She wanted to out-do her survivor mother in the area of the Holocaust.

As I write this, it still sounds bizarre, yet this is exactly what happened. As her daughter, I was embarrassed. I didn't quite understand why she was so angry or more to the point, what I had to do with it, or what I could possibly do to change things. That wasn't my job, but I didn't know that then. I felt weirdness about all of it. I now know these feelings to be born from shame. I was a kid (and later a teen) and didn't have the tools or ability to fix anything that had happened in the past—and I didn't know that this wasn't even possible. So I continued to feel icky—for lack of a better word—about all of it.

Of course, as the grandchild of my Bubby and Zeidy, I felt an enormous amount of pride. When you hear people discuss your grandparents' histories using words like "miraculous" and "brave" and "unbelievable," how could you not feel proud? They were special. Their stories were special. Not many people had experienced what they had experienced, and even fewer had lived to tell about it. So it stood to reason that my family was special, that I was special. After all, were it not for my grandparents' survival, I would not be alive.

I was told, from my earliest days, the story of how special I was. Constantly. How amazing it was that I was alive. How I was born against so many odds. How much I could accomplish. How much I *must* accomplish because of what my grandparents had gone through decades earlier to ensure that I would someday exist. How my existence was, in and of itself, a miracle, one I could never forget or take for granted. It was a heavy load for anyone, and certainly for any child, to carry. But it was mine, and I knew it would be mine always.

I tried, mostly unsuccessfully, to reconcile the shame I felt around my mom's experience with the pride I felt about the miracle from which I was born. Even at a very young age, I knew there was something enormously different—and complicated—about all of this. I didn't have the language or the maturity to understand it, but I had the awareness. Much later, other 3Gs told me of their similar experiences, of the simultaneous pride and pressure that came with being the great hope and triumph of the family. As the years went by, I learned that pride was a double-edged sword. With it, in many families (like mine), came angst and conflict and unresolved issues. In my own family, the Holocaust and my grandparents' story were almost "too" out there, too exposed, if that were possible. We had almost *too many* books lying around the house on Hitler, on the Lodz Ghetto, on the Final Solution. Later, we also had *too many* VHS tapes with recordings of my grandmother's powerhouse speeches for group after group, audience after audience. It was *too often* the topic of conversation with just about anyone.

Was it too much? Yes, absolutely. I felt different from my friends. I felt that it was always addressed in some way or another in every situation, even the ones most removed from it. I knew I was supposed to be enormously proud, but I kind of wished it would just go away—or at least fall more into the background.

There were two parallel worlds simultaneously coexisting in our home, in our lives. We lived in a big house on a wide, quiet street in a suburb with a well-regarded name. We had luxury cars in the driveway, and we were usually among the first to have the latest "must-haves" from an Atari to a VHS player to HBO. Yet, no matter how successful my father was in business or how many fur coats my mom possessed (this was the '80s, remember), we always, always had these totally familiar, but, let's face it, *weird* books and conversations going on inside our walls. We had the never-ending "keeping up with the Joneses" mentality on one hand, and yet, at least some of us were still one degree removed from Auschwitz on the other.

Regular, everyday conversation had almost too many little, Holocaust-related mentions or inclusions that, now, remind me of the significant juxtaposition of everyday-ness and pure horror: "*That German Shepherd the neighbor was walking reminds me of the dogs Mengele had with him on the platform at Auschwitz.*" Or, "*Your eyes look like my sister's. Did you know that after my mother sent her away before the war, we never saw her again?"* To this day, I cannot eat a baked potato without my grandmother's voice in my head saying, *"Alkele,"* [her loving nickname for me, roughly translated to mean "little Allie"] she would say, *"I risked my life to steal potatoes in the ghetto. I had no choice. I knew I had to come back with something for my brother."*

I wasn't there when it all happened, but I was immersed in it.

PEOPLE ASK ME, YOU KNOW... I GO AROUND AND TELL MY stories in synagogues and in high schools and in universities and when there is a question and answer period, they ask me, "How did you survive?"

And my answer is, "I don't know myself."

I don't know how I survived.

Probably I survived because I must be here to tell the story. There must be somebody here to tell the story so people cannot deny it later. And I am a real survivor. I am an eyewitness of the atrocities. That's maybe why I survived. But I didn't work towards it to know if I will go to the right or the left. This will be better or this will be better. Nobody knew what to do or how to do it. It just so happened.

And if the war would go on two more days, I wouldn't be sitting here and talking about the story. I wouldn't be here.

~ Paula Dash, 1992

‡

Aftermath

What I have learned is that when it came to their histories, there were varying degrees to which Holocaust survivors were and are able to share their stories. Some were silent, sullen and totally closed about what had happened to them. Others, like my survivor grandparents, were open, expressive and almost free-flowing about it. It was who they were, why they were here. When I was older and learned that "the story" was a no-no as far as discussion in some survivor families, I was fascinated: *You mean that this is something some people don't talk about? Wow.* Clearly that was not the case with my people. For my grandmother, her story was, I believe, the key to her freedom and salvation in life. It was precisely because of telling the story that she was able to process and live with what she had experienced.

Everything, from the mundane (such as, "What's for dinner?") to the important (such as whom I'd marry), carried with it a thread of the Holocaust. It isn't too much to say that the Holocaust was like a member of the family, a bigger, stronger, more powerful member whose presence was always felt. A member that took a whole lot out of each and every one of us.

When I was ten, I couldn't complain about the major (MAJOR!) mistake I made when I tried to cut my own hair, because at least I wasn't sent to Auschwitz where my head would be shaved to the point of pain and bleeding.

When I was fourteen, I was told I couldn't complain about the pains of having a younger, clingy, eight-year-old sister, because…well, you know, I was lucky to have a sister who wasn't sent to the gas chamber.

When I was in high school, I lied to my parents, telling them that a boyfriend whose last name was "Isaacs" was Jewish, when I knew full well he wasn't. Meanwhile, by that point, my parents believed they'd safely deposited me into a Jewish day school, complete with Jewish History classes and of course, all Jewish classmates.

When I was a freshman in college, I couldn't talk about any friends or—gasp!—any boyfriends who weren't Jewish, because, of course, only fellow Jews could be relied upon and trusted.

When I was in my early twenties and starting to make my own way in the world, I knew that failure or even stumbling was not an option, because my grandparents endured and survived so that I could go on and be wildly successful at everything I did. So I didn't tell my family how wrong my big ad agency job was for me or how uncertain I was about my future.

Later, when I started to talk to other 3Gs, oftentimes I heard the same variations of this story over and over: *"You can't be sick! You have the sniffles? I survived Auschwitz!"* Or, *"You don't cry when you lose a baseball game. You cry when you lose a brother in the camps."*

I began to make it a full-time job to sweep imperfection or uncertainty under the rug. I showed my best hand, so to speak, when asked about my life or a particular situation. I was full-on operating in my very controlling and controlled, very-well-thought-out brand of perfectionism, and I was perfecting even that.

Maybe my family would have been just as idiosyncratic even without the Holocaust in the picture, but it's not possible to know. The reality was that it was not just part of the picture; it was the picture itself. The entire thing.

As a young girl of five or six, I spent many hours of at least several years staring at the wall in the waiting room of my mother's therapist. One hour, maybe more, sitting still and quiet, without book or television (and long before the days of handheld electronics or anything portable that could remotely entertain a kid of that age) or any other diversion a kid might need. Confused, bored beyond words, wondering why I wasn't somewhere else. While I can't say for sure, since my mom isn't here to confirm, I do believe I was there in that waiting room for every single appointment, which would have been weekly or even more frequently. Every. Single. Appointment.

Mom, generally unable—or perhaps unwilling—to break any cycles or move forward, used her time with this doctor and others to befriend and convince them why her victimhood was so insurmountable, all the while having a child in tow who could, and should, have been elsewhere. She was with that particular therapist, Dr. Feldstein (not his real name), for years, eventually leaving him because he urged her to take some responsibility and learn to forgive. I couldn't hear it all through those walls, but I got the gist: He wanted her to get her stuff together, and she preferred, instead, to dwell on it indefinitely. Even at that young age, I knew on some level that I wasn't supposed to be there, and that what my mom was doing there wasn't something positive or productive. This was one of the earlier instances in which my view of myself as more of a caretaker, as the more mature one, as someone who could fix things, began to form. If I could control this and make it better, the problems would go away. But only if I could make sure I was perfect and without any issues, could I fix everyone else. It was a burden I treated like a strength. As a kid, I didn't know how inappropriate or unrealistic the situation or my thinking around it was. And like so many other things of this nature, it took me decades to begin to unravel my faulty thinking around this so that I could begin to undo it.

Years later, as an adult, I was a caretaker of my grandmother. The generation that separated us—namely, my mom—was gone. My grandmother had brought me up, and now it was my turn to take care of her. It was my job to fix whatever I could, so that her life would be as comfortable and easy (and affordable) as possible. I spent many, mostly frustrating, hours corresponding with bureaucrats from the German government, trying to convince them—with the help of doctors and my grandmother—of Bubby's profound post-traumatic stress disorder, so that they would increase the monthly amount of reparation and pension money she received from them. These reparations were basically the,

Aftermath

"We're sorry we sent your family to the gas chamber, but here is some money to make it better" gestures, and the whole process really made me mad. In my twenties and thirties, I had become something of a secretary to Bubby, not just managing her correspondence and her administrative life from bills to service calls to trips to renew her driver's license, but also becoming her advocate with anyone who denied her what she wanted or needed, such as, in her eyes, the German government.

To this day, I still have the "Bubby Germans" folder in my files, despite having no need for it anymore. I can't bring myself to throw out those letters and receipts of restitution payments. They serve as a reminder, one of injustice and frustration and compassion and overwhelm and now, a reminder to me that I'm not always in control, and that's OK.

Perhaps understandably, I have found some answers and comfort in the twelve-step model many alcoholics and addicts turn to for their healing. Growing up with all of that Holocaust all around me took its toll, one that waited years to reveal its true legacy. The year 2009 began a period of enormous introspection and transformation for me, including but not limited to my divorce from my kids' father. Around that same time, I began to devour the teachings of these programs and still do, at times. There were (and are) cycles to break, and no one else had broken them for me (nor are they ever going to). No, alcohol wasn't our issue; the Holocaust was. Without getting too much into the language of these patterns and ways of being, it started to become clear that I wasn't alone as far as feeling after-effects of the way I grew up. But I also began to wonder things like, *Would alcohol have been easier to deal with?* Perhaps more accepted or understandable.

Regardless, the fallout of being the grandchild and daughter of this history was just as all-encompassing. There was an aftermath to wade through, and that aftermath was my life. I didn't want to die like my mom at the age of fifty-one and a lifelong victim who'd never fulfilled her enormous potential. As I get closer to that age, I wonder what there is beyond fifty-one and wonder if I will get any chances beyond that. I've told myself countless times that it's "too late" to do something, that I'm "too old," that fifty-one is coming up just around the corner. Then, equally as many times, I have reminded myself what Bubby showed me about strength and character. How she emerged as a butterfly in her seventies and eighties. How anything is possible when you shift your perspective and remember to be grateful for all of it.

‡

Throughout the process of interviewing approximately 150 other adult 3Gs over the period of a year or two, I found insight and comfort learning that I was not the only one who'd grown up feeling the way I did and that as an adult, I wasn't the only one revisiting and evaluating what it all meant. Some, though not all, also explained situations in which they, too, were caretakers of sorts for the adults around them and for their stories, and that I wasn't the only kid who grew up in a family that was more chaotic than peaceful. If you do the math, you will see that those my age are at the upper end of this group. What I have found is that the older the 3G, the more likely he or she is to live near and often be very intertwined with his or her survivor grandparent(s). In fact, the closer the 3G is to my own age, the more likely it is that his or her grandparent-survivors lived nearby and were, for the most part, a core part of the nuclear family as opposed to a holiday-only kind of grandparent.

For kids seeking love and closeness (and which kids aren't?), this had some wonderful benefits. Growing up in true proximity to my grandparents and virtually being raised by my relatively young grandmother was a true gift that not only shaped who I became, but one that I carry with me, gratefully, always. The love that surrounded me, the undivided time and attention I received, the adventures I had—it may have been taken for granted at the time, but I now know how truly fortunate I was. I look at my own kids, now young adults, and feel sadness that they will have never known that feeling of being the most loved and cherished grandchild in the world. Of the two grandparents they knew in person, one lived across the world and the other in another state. They never had the singular experience of having a Bubby make them a (terrible) school lunch with some sort of pickle-and-chicken concoction smushed into a brown paper bag or pick them up after Hebrew school in an oversized Cadillac. They never worried about running into their Zeidy at the JCC while hanging out with their friends as he was holding court, sharing his story of survival to strangers in the room with the vending machines.

No, they would never know any of that. A gift they didn't receive, though one we may share when they have their own kids. By the same token, they also haven't known of the boundary issues. I was careful not to tell them what I felt was inappropriate for a child to know. I never dragged them to a therapy appointment—in fact, I was so sensitive about not forcing them to do things that I rarely ever went on any errands while they were with me. I was intent on letting their free time be their free time, and I went grocery shopping while they were in school or elsewhere. I never would have asked them to fight my battles with the German government or anyone else. I've impressed upon them countless times—especially following my divorce from their father—that their parents' happiness is in no way their responsibility or burden. Not now, not ever. They've never been subjected to a fight between a parent and a grandparent. Once would have been hard to take; many over the course of years would have been to them, as it was to me, pure trauma.

They've never felt any great responsibility, whether with pride or burden or a combination thereof, to carry a legacy or pass something on. They bear no story, and they take care of no one else. Almost to an extreme, perhaps. They know very roughly what happened to Bubby, and they had her in their lives enough so that they both remember her, but they aren't a receptacle for the details of the story. They haven't grown up hearing about the Lodz Ghetto or stealing the potatoes in the dead of the night or of years of starvation or of seeing your mother be led to a certain death. They haven't had to rifle through books with dead corpses to find a magazine or school paper they were looking for. They haven't had an innocent question about hair or food answered with a Holocaust reference. The story is part of their family history. It is not, however, their present; nor is it their responsibility.

The closeness, the all-encompassing relationship, the unconditional love I experienced in my relationship with my Bubby and Zeidy gave them more power over my life than the typical grandchild and I, in return, knew I owed them far more than the typical grandchild might. Take all of this and combine it with the superstar status that had been bestowed upon me as the first grandchild and the only family member born in America, and the one that had all the goods and the tools to take the family forward and do everyone—including all the dead relatives, I suppose—proud. It was a lot for any kid to manage.

At the same time I was growing up, Bubby's star was rising. Meanwhile, Mom's wasn't.

It was confusing. On one hand, I was supposed to feel lucky, blessed and grateful even to be here. On the other hand, there was always, for me, a lot of angst, confusion and questions.

CHAPTER 3
THE TRIP

March 1994

Following my college graduation in 1993, I was living in New York City, enjoying all that the "big city" had to offer. I'd always dreamed of moving to the Big Apple, and I'd arrived. I had an important-sounding job ("Assistant Media Planner") in a top advertising agency. It was the kind of job that my parents and I boasted to others about but that paid next to nothing, that viewed "nine-to-five" as part-time and that, alas, bore no resemblance to anything that interested me. It sounded impressive, but I was miserable.

Not surprisingly, after less than a year, I'd decided I wanted out of the ad agency. I didn't know what was next, but I knew that if I could come up with a good project or something interesting to do during the break between this job and whatever came next, quitting would end up looking like a brilliant decision to everyone else. Around the same time, the movie, *Schindler's List*, was all the rage, and Steven

Spielberg's Shoah Foundation was being established. Just two years before, in the spring of my junior year at Penn, I'd arranged for my grandmother to come to Philadelphia and speak to my Literature of the Holocaust classmates. This was the first time in my adult life that I had sought out or displayed my Holocaust family connection on my own volition. It was a turning point for me and now, everywhere I looked, I was getting Holocaust messages. The stories were becoming more important in the eyes of mainstream America and all the more so, as now the survivors themselves were getting older and passing away.

Suddenly, it seemed acceptable—and interesting—to have a personal association to the Holocaust.

In the midst of all of this, it came to me.

I knew what my "Meantime Project" would be.

If Spielberg could do it, well then, maybe so could I. Of course, my version would likely come with less bells and whistles and more...family dynamics.

I'd travel to Poland and Germany with my mom and my grandmother, a trip of three generations to find facts, make memories and maybe even connect in new ways to one another. A few years before, in 1991, my mom and grandmother had travelled on such a trip together and both had wanted me to join them then. My grandmother was being recognized by the mayor of Bremen, a city in Germany in which she'd done hard labor during the last part of the war. While it was a great honor, at that time I had no interest in leaving my college social life for a Holocaust-centered trip to Eastern Europe. Now, three years later, the stakes were different: I needed an out from the job I couldn't bear, and I knew my mom was eager to take the trip again, this time with me also along for the ride.

I knew exactly what my "out" would be.

Brilliant.

I couldn't wait to tell the family.

May 1994

THE THREE OF US WERE IN THE AIRPORT IN WARSAW, Poland. We—Bubby, my mom, and I—were trying to figure out which line we needed to get into so that we could get whatever passport stamps or permission we needed to leave the country. It wasn't clear where we needed to go, and it was loud and chaotic. There were hundreds, maybe thousands, of teens and young adults of every nationality, all of whom seemed to be at some stage in their group tour of Poland. They all sat on the floor in their packs, so that there was no way we could tell where—or if—one line started and another began. And even if we could tell, there was no way to get there—the floor was covered with circles of these young travelers sitting, some lying down, others sprawled out every which way.

We three stood in place in a spot right before the chaos began and surveyed the scene. We were frozen at the border of floor and massive throngs of people. It didn't seem clear as to how or even if we would be able to take care of our business and leave the country in an efficient manner.

Aftermath

"Fifty years ago, they couldn't wait to get rid of us; now we can't figure out how to leave," Mom quipped. *"Stupid Polish people. The only time they were efficient and organized was when the Germans were running the show."*

She made a lot of comments like these, my mom. She was funny and smart, and could be sarcastic, biting, even inappropriate. My adult self, a big believer in finding something humorous even in the least-humorous things, thinks these comments are pretty darn funny. Heck, my self of today might even make such a comment in a situation like this. My early twenties self, who had little perspective and didn't understand why she was always so angry and outspoken, ignored them and hoped no one else had heard her, silently thankful for the massive din from the hordes of young travelers whose voices drowned out just about everything else.

Bubby did not acknowledge Mom, nor did she look at either of us. She continued to stare straight ahead, taking in the scene and the noise and the chasm between where we stood and where we needed to pass through. She tilted her head, squinted her eyes a bit and moved her lips, as if rehearsing some sort of speech or reciting words. Then, she closed her mouth, brought her head back up straight and turned, addressing both of us:

"These are the people who killed my family," she said, surveying the Polish airport personnel with the resolve and gravitas of a five-star general. *"They starved us in the ghetto and stuffed us into the cattle car. I won't wait in their lines again."*

It was precisely in situations like these that I didn't try to argue with Bubby. Of course, these relatively young personnel were not the people who incarcerated and killed Jews, but I wasn't going to go there—not here, not now. And with that, Bubby forged forward, directly stepping into the throngs of waiting, sitting people. Mom and I had no choice but to follow suit, protesting at what we saw as a mistake. I was mortified—*You can't cut in line! You can't make a spectacle of yourself! What if we get in trouble?*

Bubby ignored both of us and continued to move forward, step by step, making her way closer to a man in a uniform who would stamp our passports and send us on our way out of this gray country full of memories. The sitting kids started to notice her and her two followers, and instead of asking questions or blocking our way, they actually began to shift over, creating a pathway for us. Perhaps not unlike Moses parting the Red Sea, Bubby began to part the way right there in the Polish airport, fully confident despite our protests.

In my mind, the walk through the people took time, but in reality, it was probably all of thirty seconds. No one cared, and no one stopped us. We got our stamps with a smile and were merrily on our way to the next leg of the trip: Germany. We began to laugh about the experience and Bubby's bold solution immediately, while she smiled at her own ingenuity and bravery. This was a woman who, fifty years after the fact, decided she'd had enough of the rules and the bans and the barricades. This time, and for the last time, Bubby left her home country proudly and on her own terms.

Aftermath

‡

As far back as I can remember, my grandmother, Bubby, was a regular on the Holocaust speaking circuit, wowing and amazing audiences in churches, schools, Rotary club meetings and even the White House. She'd started around the late '70s or early '80s, which is why my memories always include her speaking engagements. No matter how many times she told the same story with the same details, she never seemed to tire or ever be overwhelmed by it. For every one of these talks, no matter who the audience, she brought with her the same composition notebook with its black-and-white-marbled cover, filled from start to finish with her story, in her words, written out in pencil, in her European script.

Bubby was a natural who also had incredible material to work with. And she felt with rock-solid certainty that hers was a story that everyone needed to know—and her audiences agreed. For years, she'd receive letters from people throughout the United States who had heard her speak, some telling her how they'd never before heard of the Holocaust or met a Jewish person, and that her story had changed their lives. Later, after the U.S. Holocaust Museum opened in the 1990s, she'd also get letters from total strangers who had picked up her "identification card" and wanted to tell her how moved they were by her story and how happy they were to know she was still alive and well.

Although my grandfather, Zeidy, died when I was still in

college, I knew from a much-earlier age that he had nowhere near the force of personality that so epitomized Bubby. Even while he was alive, Bubby was the one whose story of survival took precedence. As far as I know, he never spoke of his story publicly or in any organized way. Toward the end of his life, as he spiraled deeper into dementia, he'd throw out sentences here and there that I understood, but that had no context.

"*I was forced to eat only grass, Alkele,*" he'd say.

"*I know, Zeidy. You told me,*" I'd say, embarrassed to be scolding him; more embarrassed to be reminded of such horrors by a senile old man.

Bubby's stories were always clear and detailed. She never used a comment like, "*I don't remember*" or, "*I don't know.*" Never. She remembered everything, and she shared all of it. When I think of Zeidy, I think of him as smaller than Bubby, both literally and figuratively, relegated to the sidelines, more an observer than a participant, even though I know his experiences were as harrowing and his survival as miraculous as hers. She and her experiences were front and center, every detail recalled and shared in a way that was, truly, unforgettable for anyone listening. She was a brilliant orator and storyteller, and he could not—so did not—compete. Her English was clear and her accent easy to understand, while his was heavy and his words more simple. She managed to wear her tragedy almost easily and knew how to share it without being depressing or negative. She wasn't just positive or optimistic; she was someone whose positivity and optimism were magnetic. You could not help but feel what she felt after you'd heard what she endured. She was one of those everyone-who-meets-her-loves-her kinds of people. She'd slip in and out of "Holocaust Survivor" mode seamlessly, easily chatting and laughing about something mundane in the car on the way to or from the speech, even if in the middle of the two car rides she'd told an audience about riding for two days stuffed in a cattle car to Auschwitz. She'd always been able to be both people at once: the young, Polish-born Jewish woman who'd experienced life-and-death situations that most people knew about only from history books and the loving, attentive, totally present, almost-Americanized grandmother who wanted nothing more than to spend time with the loves of her life, her granddaughters.

She was good at both—at being a grandmother and at being a witness to history. As far as the latter, she knew how to transport an audience back with her in time and place. Her words, there in that handwritten composition notebook, were simple and bare, but the story was beyond this world. People of all ages were mesmerized, moved, floored. Some had never heard about the Holocaust and had certainly never met a survivor before. Many of those had only heard of Jews previously; she was the first they'd seen with their own eyes. She'd given herself a big job, and she did it well. Each and every time. It never seemed to be too big nor too much for her, and she never doubted her ability to tell the story in a way that would never be forgotten.

As a child, I didn't question how she managed to do this, to go to these speaking events so often (or so it seemed to me) and to perform so well. I don't think I even wondered why she was doing this or if this was "normal." It was what we did, part of our family story, our routine. Bubby was a speaker, and she talked about the Holocaust, that much I knew for sure. Bubby's speeches were regular occurrences, and while I must've known that accompanying one's grandmother to a speech about the Holocaust wasn't exactly the most normal or common grandparent/grandchild outing, it was what we did, and I don't recall ever questioning it. She didn't seem to seek it out, the invitations or the attention. It all came to her. In my younger years, it seemed that she was always booked solid, and appeared to accept this as her lot, more responsibility than burden. She did what she did without much discussion. Some Nanas and grandkids went to the park or out to lunch, maybe at a club. My Bubby and I went to junior colleges and the Rotary Club. They were waiting for her; we had no choice.

My mom, too, had a story to tell. It was a different kind of story, though. It wasn't eagerly awaited by audiences from near and far, and it wasn't one whose sharing was encouraged. Despite being surrounded during her childhood and even beyond by other survivor families, she felt more of an outcast, full of shame and confusion than someone who was proud to tell a story. In the 1950s, '60s and '70s, my mom and other "2Gs" like her did not bond over their stories or even openly discuss the similarities among their parents. They didn't talk about it even though it was the single-most defining aspect of their lives. The quirks, funny sayings and Old

Aftermath

World ways that they may have shared today via Facebook or Meetup groups or even one-on-one conversation simply did not have a place in the dialogue of those years. Surviving the Holocaust was, then, something to keep to yourself and maybe even be ashamed of. The children of these survivors lived with it every day but had little to no chance to process any of it. Beyond the natural human need to share her story, my mom, I now know, deeply craved the kind of attention and adoration that her mom received from strangers, audiences and people everywhere. She would have liked to have had a mother focused on her, not one focused on putting food on the table (my grandparents owned and spent long hours at a convenience store in downtown DC in the early years) or in later years, with meeting people in audiences. They were working hard to make a living and, I suppose, to put their trauma behind them. Being the 1950s' or '60s' version of a "helicopter parent" or anything like it just wasn't happening here.

An only child, my mother was left to her own devices more often than not. As an adult, and likely as her identity began to emerge into her adulthood, she had more autonomy but still no outlet until later on when books like *Children of the Holocaust* (1979) and movies like *Schindler's List* (1993) came into the mainstream. While some people would use these early frustrations and uncertainty to become stronger and more driven in life, my mom was never able to totally move past all of it. She wanted to be loved for the story, for her knowledge of it and for her ability to live in it and come from it.

Yes, the Holocaust was my Bubby's badge of honor. My mom, meanwhile, spent her life trying to get a piece of that badge for herself. I was born in 1971, just as the complexity of this mother/daughter relationship was growing deeper and starting to emerge. I knew we were affected, even damaged, from this past. It was clear, and I saw how it affected everyone differently. My grandmother was empowered by it and in turn, was able to inspire others. My mother was drained and damaged by it and in turn, lashed out at others, most often her mom. Those were the energies constantly surrounding me. The Holocaust, or rather, the story of the Holocaust, was everything. It made us who we were, all of us, and it was present always and for everything. I didn't live it, I wasn't there and I wasn't a survivor. But my entire life was steeped in its aftermath.

‡

April 1994

AS I THOUGHT MORE ABOUT MY "BRILLIANT" EASTERN EUrope trip idea, I began to have some concerns. I knew what kind of family we were (and weren't). Our baggage, so to speak, was tattered and bulky and heavy as hell. And deep down, I must have known without a doubt that we were not, by any standard, the kind of family that could go on such a trip and come out of it closer or better. We always fought.

Aftermath

I've since, in my research for this book, seen many videos of these powerful and life-affirming, multigenerational trips to Poland and Lithuania and elsewhere in Eastern Europe. While I could relate to the discoveries and the emotions of the family members, I'd look at the way the experience strengthened already-loving families, and I wondered what might've been different in our case.

Nevertheless, I forged ahead, determined to make it happen.

‡

Lodz, Poland
May 1994
Any time I would meet someone—usually an elderly person with what I learned to be the telltale survivor accent and similar disposition, maybe an arm tattoo as well—who said they were from Lodz, I'd excitedly tell my grandmother I met someone from her city (a "landsman" was the term in Yiddish).

"Oyyy!" she'd invariably spit. *"Ask them what street they lived on. I don't think they were from Lodz. They were probably from a little village outside of Lodz."*

"But Bubby," I'd say, *"they said specifically they were from Lodz. People don't make that kind of stuff up."*

"No," she was adamant. *"Everybody wanted to be from Lodz, but most weren't."*

To Bubby, coming from Lodz was a status symbol, not unlike Beverly Hills or Paris, perhaps. And when I mentioned that it was, after all, a city in Poland, a country and a place not exactly known for its beauty or cosmopolitan appeal, she would stare blankly at me as if I were an alien experiencing its first day on Planet Earth. *"Alkele,"* she would say, *"what are you talking about?"*

And the conversation would be over.

When I saw Lodz for myself, I was neither over- nor underwhelmed. It was not unlike many other Eastern European cities at that time or even fifty years prior. In its way, it was bustling, streets and sidewalks teeming with men and women whose faces revealed little and whose determined gaits appeared intense. In another way, it seemed empty and almost dead.

It was gray. Very, very gray. There was to my eye no beauty, nothing distinct, no personality. It could have, and maybe should have, felt depressing, but it was more neutral than anything else. There was nothing about Lodz that felt good or bad, strange or home-like. It was just a place where people lived, worked, walked, drove and rode buses. I didn't feel any connection to it, even though generations of my DNA had originated from this place. Ugly may be too harsh a word, but to me, even as I think about it over two decades later, I recall that there was nothing *not* ugly about it.

Of course, Bubby didn't like my assessment. To her, Lodz represented everything beautiful—and innocent—about life before the war. She truly seemed to be wearing rose-colored glasses while back on her home turf. Like the parent who refuses to acknowledge a misbehaving child or a spouse blind to a partner's flaws, she saw beauty and love in every corner. All I could see was blah and more blah. I admired—and was amused by—her steadfast defense of a city she still loved, despite the reality and the history. I, on the other hand, struggled mightily and ultimately fruitlessly, to see what she saw.

WE CAME INTO THE GHETTO AND WE WERE ASSIGNED A little room, [the] size [was] about sixteen by eighteen or so. Just one little room for all six people. And there are new laws that we cannot go out. It is a curfew after five o'clock. We cannot go out. And the conditions there are very, very, very bad. Horrible. We did not have running water. We had to go for a bucket of water about three or four miles. And there were hundreds of people there.

The Nazis gave us rations. Every ten days we got a little, an eighth of a round bread. An eighth of a piece. An eighth of a portion of bread. We got two or three potatoes. We got a little sugar. A little brown oil. And a little salt. And that was all for ten days. People ate the piece of bread up as soon as they came home with it, so naturally a great starvation... A great percentage of starvation set in the ghetto. People swell up. They had the water bags under their eyes. Swollen legs.

Every day that we survived the day in the ghetto was a miracle that we survived it.

~ Bubby on G. Gordon Liddy's radio show

‡

Aftermath

Wherever we went on those Polish streets, we'd attract a crowd. Today, the Polish people are probably far more used to seeing Americans visiting the same places over and over in an attempt to make sense and find some answers. But in 1994, we were on the earlier end of this trend and seeing us in our very obviously non-Polish clothing and with a video camera, the people were curious. Whenever they'd start to follow us around or look at us, my grandmother would talk to them, in Polish. The kids would usually giggle and run off, making way for adults of all ages. She particularly wanted to talk to the older adults and wasn't about to let them get off so easily. She'd ask them questions about how long they'd lived in Lodz and if they remembered the war. The people were friendly and open, answering her questions with lengthy answers and stories. Once Bubby had ascertained that they did indeed remember the war years, she'd go further: "*Do you remember the Jews? What happened to all the Jews who lived here?*"

Then the conversation would inevitably take a different turn. The body language would change, and even though I didn't understand the words, I understood the change that was taking place. "*We don't remember the Jews,*" they said. Or, "*The Jews left; they wanted to leave,*" they explained. And my personal favorite: "*We loved the Jews. We wish they would've stayed.*" No one spoke the truth; all was feigned innocence and ignorance.

I'd urge Bubby to not pursue this line of questioning. I felt strange and embarrassed. I didn't want these people to know we were Jewish, and I certainly didn't want to alienate anyone. I felt a blanket hatred toward this country (never mind that this was a pretty irrational way of looking at things), but I didn't want to confront these individual elderly people. For what? They certainly weren't fans of Jews, but the last thing they wanted to discuss was the fate of the Jews all those years before. But she wouldn't listen to me. She asked all of them the same questions, even if she got the same answers. Maybe she needed to make a point, to be vindicated. I'd known this woman long enough to know she wouldn't be swayed once she was on a roll.

After Bubby made her way through the pockets of people stopping to stare at us and answering her probing questions, Bubby led us to a house in another part of what used to be the ghetto. We stopped in front of a house, a small, neat house with a little garden area in front.

"*This is it, Alkele,*" she said, turning to me. "*This is the home I told you about. This is where Hans Biebow, the Nazi who was in charge of the ghetto, lived. This,*" she said, swiveling to point at the small grounds by the house, "*this is where I came in the middle of the night to steal the potatoes to keep my family alive.*" This was a story I knew. Her parents and her brother, Henry, were starving to death. The small rations of some bread each week and some watery soup each day were not nearly enough for anyone. My grandmother was not one to idly sit by and allow things to happen to her; she was someone who took matters into her own hands, even when it seemed there were no options and she had no control over anything. She was something of a go-getter in the ghetto. She'd always had a job, which was no easy feat. She'd lived with her family as a teenager for a few years in Berlin, and she spoke a perfect German, like a native German, she always liked to tell me. Because of her superior skills as a seamstress (which I believe saved her life, ultimately), she always had not only a little extra food but a little extra intelligence about what was going on or how to make some things happen.

She knew the Germans had food. This man, Hans Biebow, had potatoes growing in front of his house.

THEN ONE DAY WHEN WE WERE OUT OF RATIONS, WE *didn't get any food anymore, it was a chaos in the ghetto. It was terrible. Didn't get any food. And I worked. At my place of work, I went to the window and looked down and I saw potatoes growing there. The potatoes were planted by the head of the "Kripo." That's Criminal Police, shortened. Kripo… And it was a big field of potatoes. And I looked down and I said to myself, "Oh. They are potatoes. At night I am going to come here and dig out some potatoes."*

And they were very, very dark nights. It was around July. And I needed something to eat for my brother. And also for my mother. And I went. It was very dark. I took a sack and I took a cleaver to dig. And I went there. If I would have been caught, I wouldn't have been shot because this was such a beast, this [man]. He would cut me up in pieces. But I risked my life and I dug the potatoes and put it in the sack and I tore off the greens to get the potatoes and I went home about four or five blocks. I took it on my shoulder. And we lived in the first floor. I opened the window from the outside and dumped the potatoes in. Then I looked up in the sky and it was still night. It is still dark. I go and take the rest of the potatoes. So I went back and took the rest. And after the potatoes, there were some other, the green… I forgot the name of it. Rutabagas. Yes. I took this and came home. And dumped it. And this was in July, the last of July. And it lasted us a few days and then we had to go. Then

Aftermath

we had to go out of the ghetto and leave the potatoes and everything. Anyway…we went to Auschwitz.

Looking at his house now, I see how he lived compared to the Jews. His house was not unlike a nice, neat, suburban-type house in America, on a quiet street with green grass and birds chirping (literally). Bubby and her family, on the other hand, were in another part of the walled-off ghetto in a tiny, stuffy room, with anywhere from one to three families packed in like the starving prisoners that they were. During the latter part of their incarceration in the Lodz Ghetto, Bubby's father died before her eyes, a once strong and vibrant man weakened and ultimately killed by starvation and tuberculosis. Such were their conditions over a relatively long period of time, for three to four years.

On one particular night, she'd had enough. Maybe something new happened that day, but more likely she got to a tipping point. Back then, as now, she wasn't someone who found it easy to lie back and take whatever life put in front of her. As in the airport, when she parted the throngs of teens as if she were Moses crossing the Red Sea, she decided to do whatever she could to take matters into her own hands. There was no part of the plan that was not dangerous. She could be caught and likely killed at any moment. The Nazis, she'd tell me, enjoyed shooting Jews and at this point, earlier on in the war, they weren't as concerned with "wasting" a bullet on a Jew as they became later in the war.

When she left that cramped, crappy, little room in the dead of the night, she was off. She says she grabbed as many potatoes as she could carry, I suppose digging up the ground with her bare hands and whatever cleaver-type tool she had.

Aftermath

I always envisioned the family eating the potatoes as they were, biting into them like they were apples or pears, and that thought always perplexed me and grossed me out a bit. I now think they were able to cook them in some way, perhaps over an open fire or in an oven-like structure, but I am not sure. After the war, she wouldn't touch a potato before it was fully peeled and without a trace of skin. For the rest of her life, no matter where she was eating, there would be a pile of potato skins discarded on her plate.

Standing there and sharing space with that onetime field of potatoes on that quiet, sunny day, I was finding it hard to reconcile the story I'd always heard with the visual reality of what stood before me in the place where it had actually happened. In some ways, I felt like I was on a walking tour of a historical place like Williamsburg, Virginia, where I'd visited with my fourth-grade class. It was history plopped down into our modern world and despite having known the history, it seemed totally removed from all that I was familiar with.

Not only did I know the stories, but they were my stories. This was where I came from. Without Lodz, there was no me. I may have been a twenty-something college graduate living the fun life in New York City, but I came from Lodz. And yet, being here, standing here on a gorgeous, late spring day with people from the 1990s all around us, it didn't feel like something I was actually connected to. It felt, well... weird. These Polish people had nothing to do with me. They wanted nothing to do with me or with my history. They pretended the Jews happily trotted off from Poland to some other great life somewhere else. And they let it happen. They conveniently forgot all about it. They wanted it in the past and gone already.

So I continued on, perhaps expecting some sort of sign of the bolt-of-lightning variety to show me I was in the right place, that this was my place; maybe that it remembered me, that it welcomed me. But I didn't find it in those apartment courtyards where Bubby was questioning old and poor Polish people about their actions or whereabouts fifty years earlier. I certainly didn't find it on the streets with the gray-looking people walking, determined and emotionless, to work or home. I didn't even find it in the former Nazi's yard of the potatoes. I wondered if I would find such a connection or sign at all. Or if this was silly, and my expectations had been inordinately lofty. After all, I'd used this trip as an excuse to quit my ad agency job. What did I think was going to happen? Just be happy to be here, I tried to remind myself. Maybe there is no bigger message or sign.

After we'd walked around the area that once housed the ghetto, Bubby wanted to take us to the place she'd lived before the war. She, of course, remembered the address (what did she not remember?) and aside from a few questions to people on the street about directions, she knew how to get us there.

Her demeanor changed as we arrived at the building. Her voice changed a little, and her body language got softer, her energy bittersweet. *"Alkele, we had a beautiful life here. This*

*is the courtyard we'd play in. My mother would make dinner
and would call to us, to all of the kids, when it was time to come
back in. Everything we needed was here, everyone we loved was
nearby."*

I tried to imagine a young Bubby with her siblings and
her friends, yelling, playing, totally free. She said she never
experienced anti-Semitism. Life was easy and full for her in
Lodz in those days; she had her school, her youth group and
her family.

*"Let's go into the building. I want to show you my apart-
ment."*

"No, Bubby, I don't want to," I said. I was fine walking
around and looking, but I started to feel very uncomfortable
doing things we weren't supposed to be doing in places we
weren't supposed to be. That was a difference between Bubby
and me: I was a rule follower, she…not so much.

When my sister was born in 1977, I was about five-and-
a-half years old. In those days, kids under a certain age were
not allowed past the waiting room. Bubby took me downtown to the Washington, DC hospital where my sister had
been born a day before. I told Bubby I'd wait while she went
back to see her daughter and her new granddaughter. I had
no desire to meet my new sister at that point, and besides,
there was a little girl around my age in the waiting room who
had some cool Barbies and wanted to play together.

But Bubby would have none of it. She insisted that I
come with her, despite my protests and despite the rules
that barred me from visiting patients or newborns. She half-

dragged me, half-held my hand normally, through the waiting room. My protests got loud enough for a guard to hear and take notice.

"*Ma'am,*" he said.

She ignored him.

"*Ma'am, you can't take her back there,*" he said a little louder.

"*See Bubby? Just leave me here,*" I said.

"*Alkele, no. You can come with me.*" She was determined and paid no mind to the guard.

At this point, he got up off his stool and tried to physically block her way.

"*Ma'am, I am going to have to call security.*"

Finally, she stopped in her tracks. She didn't like the idea that "security" had some sort of power over her, but this guard was a big man, and there was no way she was getting past him with a screaming five-year-old in tow.

In an unusual turn of events, Bubby stepped down. Really, she had no choice. She left me to play Barbies with my new friend, while she went to Mom and Erica.

‡

Back in Lodz, we approached the building.

"*Yes, this is it,*" Bubby said, repeating the address.

We looked up. It was about five stories. Dark and worn brick, a dark red bordering on brown. It looked no different than any of the buildings around it.

We all stood and looked at it, lost in our thoughts.

Aftermath

"Let's walk around," Bubby suggested.

We walked around to the side and found ourselves in a large courtyard area bordered on all sides by identical apartment buildings.

"This is where the children would play," Bubby said. *"All the kids in the neighborhood would play here for hours. Then the mothers would start to call their kids back for a meal, 'Bella! Sara!'—it would break up for a while."*

I tried to picture the fun times here. Bubby spoke with such a wistfulness, it was all I could do to imagine what this space was like in a different time. I couldn't. But I wanted to honor it. This is where my grandmother had come from. This is the place that gave her some of the happiest times of her life. She hadn't asked to leave here or to come to America. That was never her dream. America was not something people who lived quiet and content lives sought out. America was something forced on her. It was the best choice at a bad time. Not that she didn't love her adopted country—she was as patriotic and informed an American as they came. She proudly told me many times how she learned English in part from watching the televised McCarthy trials in the 1950s. She drove a Cadillac, lived in a nice condo in a high-rise building right across from the mall—but she hadn't asked for any of it. She was still a "Lodz-er" at heart.

"I want to go inside," Bubby said, breaking the silence.

I'd been worried she might say this. I was fine with looking at everything from the outside, but I started to feel really uncomfortable when, as with the impromptu interviews with any elderly Poles she saw on the street, she wanted to go further.

"I don't think that's a good idea, Bubby," I said.

She wasn't listening.

"Let's just see," she said, already turning on her heels and well on her way.

We made our way into the dark entrance. I looked around for an elevator. Of course there was none. So we started to trek our way up the stairs. They wound around the cavernous insides of the old building, each floor seeming to be about a floor and a half in regular terms. Huffing and puffing, we made our way to the third floor.

"Floor three," Bubby announced.

I had to laugh. *"Thanks, Bubby. I figured that out, too."*

It was hard to tell which door was which; nothing seemed marked clearly, and numbers were hard to come by. Bubby looked around and then picked a door.

"Are you sure you want to knock?" I asked, not sure what to expect but not feeling comfortable about any of the options.

"Of course, Alkele! What do you mean?"

Please let no one be home. Please let no one be home. Please let no one be home, I said over and over in my head.

The door opened. A woman looking to be in her late thirties with dark hair and nondescript work clothes—a blouse, a knee-length skirt, sensible shoes and thick pantyhose—answered the door, full wide, with no suspicion.

A conversation, all in Polish of course, ensued and within

seconds, we were out of the hallway and on the other side of the door.

I looked around. The place was smallish, with nothing on the walls. I couldn't believe we were in there. I was surprised at how easily and freely the woman opened the door for us and let us in, but then again, nothing on this trip, with Bubby at the helm and all of Poland at our disposal, seemed to go as planned.

The woman soon disappeared into the kitchen to prepare tea, I assumed.

We looked around. *"It's so small here, Bubby. How did your whole family live here together?"* I asked in a whisper, not that the woman understood any English anyway.

"It's because of the Communists," she said. *"They split our apartment into three. This is only one-third of where we lived. When we lived here, there was room for everyone."*

The original apartment she'd lived in with her parents and three younger siblings had been subdivided into three smaller apartments. That made more sense. The space was nondescript, but how it looked now was of no interest to Bubby anyway.

The Polish woman came out with a tray of clear glass cups, saucers and a pot of steaming tea. She placed everything down on the table where we three were sitting, and started to set up and pour.

Perhaps this was my magical moment. Perhaps this was my sign.

You are sitting here drinking tea in Bubby's old apartment in Lodz, I told myself. *You found the building, you made your way inside, and now you are looking at the same walls she and her family looked at every day for years. How much more magical does it get than this? What more do you want?*

We spoke for an hour or so with this lovely woman, who seemed (like all the Polish people we encountered) to know little about the Holocaust and the millions of Jews who had lived there prior to the war. We didn't press the issue, even when she shared her opinion that millions of Jews had left Poland willingly and proactively. She was younger, so her opinion was just that—an opinion. She'd not witnessed any of it herself. Likely, that's what she had been taught and had no reason to question it.

I kept thinking that I was sitting inside the very same walls that my great-grandparents, whom I would never know, once inhabited. I looked down from the third-story windows into the courtyard, where Bubby had said kids played for hours on end. *Bella! Sara!* I imagined the mothers, Jewish all of them in that neighborhood and that building, keeping one eye on their children, knowing they were safe, while cooking meal after meal with none of the modern kitchen tools or luxuries we have today. I thought of how difficult their job had been, yet how happy they seemed. No dishwashers or microwaves for these ladies, but only home-cooked meals every single day of every single year. Now when I think about those women, I wondered if they complained, or needed a "Moms' Night Out," or talked about balance. (I'm going to go with a "no" on both.) *First-world problems*, as people on the Internet would say. They didn't have time to complain, and they did far more with far less than people I know today.

I also thought of how none of those Jews—not the ones in the courtyard, not the mothers who watched them, not the fathers who were likely out at work or prayer—were alive anymore. I thought of my great-grandmother's own fate— a lovely life and then a train to Auschwitz where she was promptly sent to the gas chamber. It wasn't easy to marry those two parts of the same life—the tranquil courtyard view from the kitchen and the horrors of death (or even life) in Auschwitz.

I don't remember specifically what set my mother off, but there was always something. More than "something," it was really everything. She couldn't live with the Holocaust…and she couldn't live without it. And by "Holocaust," what I really mean is her mother, my grandmother. She envied the attention that the Holocaust brought Bubby, and she wanted that attention, too. She wanted to be the expert on what we were seeing. She wanted to be the translator. She wanted a different life, really. A different family history. There was yelling and blaming and accusations: *"If it weren't for you and the Holocaust, I'd have a brother or sister!"* my mom screamed to her mother. Or, *"You care more about your dead mother than you ever did about your living daughter."* There were cancelled plans and uncomfortable car rides from one Holocaust "must-see" to another.

I was a twenty-two-year-old ad agency dropout who had just been looking for an excuse to quit my job. What had started as a great excuse for a temporary break from my life brought me back to...well, exactly the place from which I came. Not Poland or Germany, per se, but the dysfunction of a family traumatized, still, by the Holocaust.

Nearly four years after returning from that trip, at the end of 1997, I became a mom. Four months after that, in April of 1998, my mom was dead. Bubby lived happily and healthily for nearly a decade more, half of that time living near me and my children, her great-grandchildren, in Florida.

I never could forget our two weeks in what is in my mind's eye a gray and sad world to which, ironically, I owe my own existence. Using the old "time plus tragedy equals humor" approach, I can now even laugh about our time there. (I cry about it, too, though much less often these days.)

After the trip, all of the many people whom I'd shared my plans with wanted to know, of course, how things went. I told them what I thought they'd wanted to hear: that it was powerful and moving and life-affirming for all of us. And that was all true. That we'd made some incredible finds and discoveries. Also true. I told everyone I was going to write a book about my grandmother, about her survival and about our trip. At twenty-three, I wasn't someone who knew a whole lot about what writing a book entailed, but I felt certain I'd figure it out and make it happen. Joke's on me, huh?

Aftermath

I took all the video footage of those two weeks and put it away in a box in a closet. Those tapes moved with me from Manhattan to New Jersey and later, to Florida. Those movies have "lived" through my marriage, the birth of my two children, my divorce and the deaths of two of the three featured characters. At some point a few years after the trip, I converted them to the more modern DVD format and then, again, promptly returned them to the closet.

As I sit here and write this in 2016, I can tell you that I have not, in the past twenty-two years, watched even one minute of that footage.

Chapter 4

SECRETS

"Is it true your grandmother is sixty-five?"

I looked up at Rose, the young lady who had been doing Bubby's nails since Bubby moved to Florida the year before.

"What?"

"Yea, she told us she was sixty-five. I thought she was maybe seventy or seventy-two, but damn, she looks good for a great-grandmother!"

I didn't even know how to answer. Here's the thing: I knew for sure Bubby was not sixty-five. She was not seventy or seventy-two, either. According to her records with the U.S. government, she was in the vicinity of eighty-seven or eighty-eight. That's a full fifteen, sixteen, seventeen years of difference. To make matters even more confusing, I'd recently learned that Bubby's younger brother, Henry, her only family member who survived the Holocaust, had handwritten a partial life story in which he listed her year of birth as five or six years earlier than her most official records, making her at that point anywhere from ninety-two to ninety-four. (Uncle Henry's short, but incredible, handwritten story also shed some light on other previously discovered stories, but we shall get to that....) Bottom line: My grandmother was anywhere from eighty-seven to ninety-four years old, and she was telling the ladies in the salon that she was sixty-five. And their only question was whether she was fudging by five or by seven years. As a point of reference, had my mother been alive at that time, she would have been fifty-eight or fifty-nine years old, and her mother was confidently sharing that she herself was sixty-five.

That her true age was rather closely hidden was a somewhat humorous, semi-open secret in our family (although Uncle Henry's disclosure made her suspected age even older than we'd thought all those years). Such subterfuge and clerical "changes" were likely not entirely uncommon in many immigrant families, as well as with women as a whole, of a certain generation. Ultimately, nothing about the story changes with her age, and if the age on its own had been the only secret, there would be no material or need for this chapter.

So, of course, there is more.

At some point, my mom started talking openly about the "big secret" of her birthday. Likely coinciding with some big breakthrough in her own life at that time, she developed an attitude, even became belligerent, about her birthday, which until then had been known to all of us as June 18, 1947.

It turns out that Mom was actually born on January 12 of that same year in the refugee camp at Bergen-Belsen. After my mom and my grandparents left the camp in 1949 or 1950, they emigrated to Israel. Zeidy had been an active Zionist before and since the war, and his heart was in the newly created state of Israel. Meanwhile, Bubby had no desire to move to what was at the time a third-world country in the desert. Moreover, her brother, Henry, had moved to Baltimore in 1948 or 1949, and Bubby's heart was there more than anywhere else. Perhaps Bubby was still shell-shocked from the war years and then from giving birth in such conditions, but somehow Zeidy won out and they went to Israel.

‡

Well after the war we lived in these houses [that had previously housed Nazis at Bergen-Belsen]. It was clean. They were fairly new, like townhouses. It was three kilometers away from the place that we were incarcerated.... We had a free life. We could go. We could travel. We went all around Germany to look for relatives because American organizations came to register people. They registered and they put the names on the wall on the outside wher-

ever they were located. And people went through and looked at the names, you know. And I was going there looking, too. I didn't expect to find my brother at all because he went to Auschwitz. He was young and he was very weak from hemorrhaging in the ghetto. I didn't expect to find him.

But people came to me that I met, that I knew, and said, "Oh, your brother. He is alive. He looks good. He is in Munich." And I didn't believe it because there were so many mistakes made. People went, they were sent to see their daughter, their sister, and it was a mistake. And it was a disappointment. And I thought this will be a disappointment, too.

But one day, I was in my little room...and this girl from downstairs came and said to me, "You know, some boys came from Munich and they want to see some girls here. Maybe you will see your brother." And I said, "My brother, I know he is not alive anymore. I know I don't have anything to look for."

She insisted, insisted and dragged me into her room. And I came into her room and there was my brother.

‡

When they moved to Israel, Bubby was miserable. It was not an easy place to live in at that time. Bubby told me she was bullied, in a way, for being "proper" and lacking that Israeli pioneer-like spirit. She'd also said that survivors, at that time, were not welcomed or treated well. I do not know if this was a common experience or more specific to her. Regardless, after a short period (a year or so), the little family of three left, likely dejected and without a great deal of hope.

Returning to Germany in order to ultimately get on a ship to the United States was easier said than done. The three had to sneak back into Germany. I don't know a ton about this part of the story and here again, there was a lot of "hush hush" whenever I asked about it. I know my mother was four years old and smuggled through mountains, and Italy, and spent at least one night in a prison somewhere (Austria or Italy, perhaps?), and Lord knows what else. I do believe that this experience—in part the actual experience that she likely remembered in bits and pieces, and in part the stories of it after the fact—affected her in what must have been a traumatic way in future years.

So back to the birthday secret: Part of making this clandestine return meant that some of their identifying information would be changed upon their re-entry to Germany. I assume that the intent was to not match identically, information-wise, with what was "on file" when they left. So, the birthdays of my grandfather (June 18) and my mother (January 12) were switched. At that same time, the family name was changed from Reich to Deich (and later to Dash when they came to the U.S.) For my mom, all of this switching around led to what I now see as her total disconnection to and ambivalence with where she had come from, how she had gotten there and ultimately, what her lot in life was. The switched birthdays, something that was certainly a not uncommon component of many immigrant families' stories, became, for my mom, a source of anger, sometimes to the point of total debilitation.

Growing up, she was six months older than she thought she was. She believed her birthday was in June, when in fact, it was in January. My mom, as did I, grew tall and developed very early on, stopping at age ten or eleven where she would be for the rest of her life. She was five feet two inches tall—petite as an adult, yet bordering-on-giant as a nine or ten year old in those years. Add to that six unaccounted-for months, and you have a girl who was literally head and shoulders above her peers. In group photos of my mom in school or at summer camp as, to use today's term, a "tween," I see a larger, unhappy-looking blonde girl who did, in fact, look out of place.

Many—and perhaps most—people would take this and live with it. They would understand that what was done, was done; that decisions were made during a tumultuous, uncertain time, and her parents did the very best they could with what they had. They were fortunate to have made it through the war, then through the DP camp, then to Israel and back, then to the U.S. (in steerage class on a ship), then to Maryland and a relatively normal life.

But not my mom. She was mad at the secret and mad at the contents of the secret.

In addition to her unhappiness over the birthday swap, my mother—as a child and later as an adult—longed for a brother or sister. She felt life would have been easier if she'd had someone with whom she could share the burden (in her view) of having parents with these experiences and of a childhood like hers. I was told that Bubby had several miscarriages before and after the birth of my mom. She never gave birth to another live child.

My mom had two first cousins who lived nearby in the Baltimore area. They were the son and daughter of Bubby's younger brother, Henry. Lenny and Shelly were my mom's first cousins, somewhat younger by eleven and nine years, respectively. What Mom (or her two cousins, for that matter) didn't know until much later, perhaps in her early twenties, was that there was one more cousin, an older brother to those two who was near the exact age of my mom. His name was Aaron.

Like Mom, Aaron was born postwar in the DP Camp at Bergen-Belsen. In a family with just two surviving members, any birth is important and all family members precious and too few. Unfortunately, Aaron had significant difficulties physically, emotionally and otherwise. He was not like other kids his age. These days, he likely would've benefitted from all sorts of early intervention therapies and other expertise, and perhaps would have been diagnosed on the Autism Spectrum. But in the 1940s and 1950s for a displaced refugee family, such options did not exist. Aaron was institutionalized in the United States around the age of four. Aaron's two younger siblings, as well as his first cousin, my mother, were never told of his existence. He was put away and not discussed. In those years and in these families that had already seen—and hidden—so much, you moved on. You kept going forward and, in those years, you did not take the time to discuss challenges and setbacks...or institutionalized children.

Aaron's younger sister, my cousin, Shelly, now a mom of three grown adults herself, has told me the story of how, at the age of thirteen, she learned for the first time that she had an older brother whose existence had never been even hinted at:

"I heard my mother in the kitchen trying to get a scholarship for a summer camp for myself and my brother Lenny. She was pleading her case and asking the party on the other line to please have compassion for a woman who was a recent immigrant with three kids. When she hung up the phone, I approached her and asked, 'Mom, why did you lie to that person and say that you have three kids when you have two?' She looked at me and said, directly, 'You have another brother, Aaron, who is twenty-one.'"

Finding out, as a teenager, that you have an older brother whose existence was literally wiped from the family conversation is, to state the obvious, a very big deal. For my mom, who was eleven years older than Shelly, learning about Aaron was a shattering experience. Remember, this was an only child of Holocaust survivors who'd grown up wishing, praying for a sibling to share the experience of these parents with. Then she learns that a cousin of the very same age—one who would undoubtedly have grown up with her side by side, comrades in arms against parents with the same history, the same quirks, the same challenges—very much exists. This discovery was a blow to her trust in her parents and to her belief in what was real, and what was not.

‡

Once, in passing, I heard mention of Bubby being "married in the ghetto." The conversation, between my mother and my grandmother, was in Yiddish and I was a bystander, not a participant.

I understood enough Yiddish at that time to glean some basics, and as soon as I piped in and asked about it, I was shushed and the conversation ended. I never asked again, and I never learned more. It wasn't something I actively recalled.

Only as I was writing this book did I learn, definitively, that Bubby did have at least one other secret she'd never shared with me or with anyone else publicly in the postwar period, as far as I knew: Bubby had been married prior to the war, happily and lovingly, it seems. The only information I have about this marriage comes, again, from the same handwritten memoir of my Uncle Henry, her brother:

Aftermath

SOMETIME IN HER MID-TEENS, POLA MET A BOY OF HER *age and they became inseparable. His name was Szlanek Pfeffer. Their relationship goes back as far as I can remember. Hardly a day went by without Szlanek being in our house and he became almost a member of our family.... [Szlanek] served 18 months in the [Polish] army. After completing his service in the army, my parents thought it was time to get married. After all, their courtship was 10 years long. Financial considerations for the future were the main obstacle. Szlanek's parents came to us and after some negotiations, a date was set for the wedding.*

Szlanek was an easygoing fellow. A furrier by trade, a terrific dancer and very likeable. He had four brothers and one sister...The brothers were tall and strong. Szlanek was rather short but ironically he was the one drafted into the Polish army, which directly led to his early demise.

~ From "The Story of My Life" by Henry Garfinkel (© 1992 / used with permission)

‡

I don't know how I would have reacted or what I would've done as far as Bubby, had she still been alive when I'd learned about Szlanek. I mean…wow. When I interviewed other 3Gs, I heard many stories of survivor grandparents who had a first spouse (and often a child, as well) before and during the war. Many of them lost their families—not just their families of origin, but their new families, too—during the war. Many of them also quickly remarried following the end of the war and started anew with that second spouse. I'd heard the stories, but I'd never before had an actual story and name to attach to Bubby's story.

By the time my grandmother and her family were forced to leave their home and move into one room in the Lodz Ghetto, Szlanek was long gone. *Bubby, how did you go on? Your husband was dead. The life you knew was gone. You were living in one room and slowly starving to death. How?* I could romanticize the relationship between Bubby and Szlanek. Sometimes I think that she went through life longing for him, still connected to him, waiting for the day when she thought they'd be reunited in death. Other times, I figured she really didn't have the time or personality to spend her living years in such a way. Bubby was a master compartmentalizer—surely she did not allow thoughts of Szlanek to cloud a life in which living in the moment was not just a theory but a full-on practice. In all likelihood, Bubby allowed herself to file Szlanek away, only to be accessed, against her conscious will, in a deep and dream-filled sleep and perhaps in an alone moment of unguarded sentiment.

When I first learned of the marriage and of the prior existence of Szlanek, I for a split second, had a romantic notion something along the lines of, *Maybe I could track down a grandchild, a descendant of Szlanek. It would be almost like finding a whole new family member.* Then I stopped, hard. How could I be so silly? Of course, he had no descendants. When you die before having children, your line dies.

Did my grandfather know about Szlanek? That I do not know. My Uncle Henry, in his handwritten memoir, did not treat the matter as if it were secret or in any way forbidden. But nonetheless, like Cousin Aaron and real ages, a secret was a secret was a secret.

‡

I met him after the liberation in Hanover. Because after the liberation, American organizations came, registered people, and they had such temporary field offices. They registered everybody, put it on a list and they hung it up on the wall. And people, the people that were liberated were going from place to place and looking up the people who were looking for families, for loved ones.

And so I met my husband in Hanover. He was with another girl, with another man. And we met and we [ask], "Where are you from?" All of us were from Lodz. So we went on, all four of us now. There were three and now there were four. And we went from city to city. And we got some bread and we got some water. And then we fell in love and we got married in a few months. October 14th [1945] we were married.

~ Bubby on first meeting Zeidy

‡

Beyond the first spouses and children who were killed, there were at times other, deeper secrets that were kept in families. My guess is that many of these secrets died with their keepers, likely never to be shared or known. My grandmother was like a vault when it came to that which she did not talk about. Almost ironically, while her story of survival was out in the open in the most public way, it was a story entirely controlled by her, down to the smallest detail. She determined what made her final version, and she shared the story in the way she wanted to share it. I remember clearly another survivor in the Washington, DC area where we lived who, like my grandmother, was popular on the speaking circuit. My grandmother would find fault with this woman's stories, detailing to my sister and me the inconsistencies in her story and the enhanced details that my grandmother did not think true.

It may seem silly, but I understood. When all you have left is your story, you want it to be right and perfect and intact. I get it.

The stories awe me. The same stories invoked anger in my mother. She felt that she lived in their shadow; I, in their incredible layers upon layers. In *The Flat*, a 2011 Israeli documentary by a 3G who, along with his 2G mother, discovered all sorts of family histories and secrets following the death of his grandmother who had fled Nazi Germany for then-Palestine in the 1930s, the narrator's mother tells her son, "*When you start looking at the past, you never know what you'll find….*"

When I think of the secrets, whether large or small, I think of loss. Lying about your age may seem funny, and heaven knows we laughed about my grandmother's ruses to keep her true age a secret for years. My sister and I still joke about it with some frequency. But the sad truth is that the lying wasn't coming from a place of vanity. It wasn't the age-lying of a once-glamorous woman clawing at the last vestiges of youth long after cosmetics or plastic surgery are options. No, it was so much more than that. And worse than that. It was the attempt of a once-helpless person to regain control over the facts of her life. It was an attempt to alter a life history that in fact had been irrevocably changed without her desire or consent. Hiding or massaging the truth was perhaps the one, last, active thing she could do after she had been rendered passive to an extreme during the most formative and important period of her life.

The secrets of my grandparents' generation were secrets born of necessity (or at least perceived necessity). The holders of these secrets had a perspective that most of us today have not lived or seen for ourselves. Whatever we (or you) think of it, none of us lived it. I try not to judge; instead I laugh when possible and, sometimes still, wonder what might've been had some parts been different.

Yet, I come to terms with the secrets and with the reality that I will never, ever know the full story. That I do not have to know the full story. That the full story, just as the sort-of-full-for-public-consumption story, does not define me as it may have defined my own mother. That without it, and its secrets, I would not be here. If anything, I am in awe of the stories and the secrets, and of the storytellers and the secret-keepers. I don't know what I would do in their shoes; I do know I would likely not be as brave or industrious. (Heck, I can't go into a restaurant that doesn't offer a gluten-free menu. I wouldn't have lasted a day in my grandparents' shoes.)

Ultimately, where my mother found resentment, I found compassion. And forgiveness. And if at all possible, some tiny semblance of understanding. I will never know what it is like to feel you need to erase the story of your first husband from your public history. I can't imagine to know what I'd feel like learning, offhandedly, that I had a brother/cousin who lived in an institution somewhere and had no clue who or even where he was. I've never lost power over my destiny. I've never had my story taken away from me. Keeping the secrets, big and small, was a way of regaining some tiny piece of control over a wildly chaotic and traumatic past. These were not secrets of deception; they were secrets of control. To live through what they lived through and to still care enough about life to want to preserve whatever shreds of control they thought they could preserve is about as life-affirming an act as I can imagine. Secrets were orderly. Secrets were manageable. Secrets were, in some way, powerful. Yes, I get it.

Chapter 5

THE GOLDEN GIRL
AND THE FAMILY HERO

I was a girl who was born into both great privilege and enormous dysfunction. I was a highly anticipated and welcomed addition to my tiny family. I was the "golden girl" my grandparents only dreamed they would live to see. Aside from marrying my dad, who was everything my grandparents had "ordered" for their daughter, I was probably my mom's best accomplishment to date. She was twenty-four when I was born.

As the first-born American on my mom's side, the enormity of what I represented to my grandparents and to my mom cannot be overstated: *You are special. You are different from everyone else. You are better. You will go further than any of us did. There is nothing you cannot do. We went through all of this so that you could be here.* These were the constant messages of my childhood. I was here, I was alive, I was an American, and it was understood that I would be perfect in every way, from how I looked to the grades I got to, later, the man I married and the children I brought into this world. In addition to my performance in school and in life, little things like my blonde hair, my movie trivia knowledge and even my football fandom had to be perfect.

‡

I was born in 1971. Gerald Ford and then, Jimmy Carter, were our presidents. Later, in the 1980s, Ronald Reagan would hold that office. In upper-middle-class suburbia, kids played actual games with balls outside, rode their Big Wheels up and down the street and waited eagerly for the Good Humor man and his telltale ringing bells announcing that ice cream was to be had. Our lives were more often than not easy and fun, devoid for the time being of complications like smartphones and Facebook. In school, we had spelling tests and a diorama book report here and there. We used encyclopedias (only at the library itself) and manual pencil sharpeners. Many of our parents smoked cigarettes freely, and their cars were often quite big.

Like many other "3Gs" who were born in the '70s, my core family unit included not just myself and my sister and our parents, but also my (maternal) grandparents. The three-generation family that had been a hallmark of the immigrant experience earlier in the century was alive and well in many survivor families. From what I learned during the 3G interviews I conducted, if the survivor grandparents didn't physically live in the same household, they often lived nearby and were present for every holiday, school event, dance recital and just about anything else a parent or grandparent might be expected to attend. In my family, it was a given that my grandparents joined our nuclear family of four in all that we did. They lived less than a half-hour away when I was younger and then, when I was in the sixth grade, my parents bought them a condo even closer, just ten minutes away.

In many survivor families, the grandparents seemed to share a feeling bordering on awe when it came to the idea of having grandkids. These were people who, for the most part, saw their families—their parents, siblings and grandparents for sure—murdered. These were people who, once the Holocaust began, doubted they would escape the same fate and never expected to live in America and bring up their own families. To say that having grandchildren was a great gift of their lives would be an understatement. And it was very different from their children—less complicated, further from the trauma, a huge future of hope rather than a past of tragedy.

Their kids, the 2Gs, never knew their own grandparents. The family experience of my generation, the generation of the 3Gs, was different. We had our grandparents. They were always nearby. They took an enormous interest in all that we did. We knew they drew much of their happiness from us, from our every little achievement. In many cases, they made us, their grandchildren, the center of their lives. (One 3G I spoke with told me that his survivor grandfather, to that day, would tell people, *I have five million dollars,* when referring to his five grandchildren.)

I knew very early on that I was the apple of my grandparents' eye. While a comfort in many ways, it was also a very high standard to maintain. If someone considers you the peak of perfection, there is little room for mistakes or—gasp!—failure. How can that be sustainable?

That said, the pleasure our grandparents took in being with us and nurturing us was for the most part a beautiful, positive part of having survivor grandparents. However, in many survivor families, there were also lingering effects of the trauma and strife of the Holocaust, which were both internal and external in nature. I saw the aftereffects of trauma expressed in my own family, in the regular shouting matches my mother would have with her parents. Clearly, there was a divide there: Mom felt cheated, that she hadn't had the childhood she deserved. My grandparents felt they did the best they could have done—and then some—given their circumstances. As an adult, I now see that the most important relationship I personally had while growing up was with my grandmother. I know that my mother dearly would have wanted such a relationship for herself, as well. But she didn't, and couldn't, and instead of cherishing what she had with her own mother, she used that relationship as an outlet for her anger.

It was within this scenario that my grandmother, even as she became a sought-after and much-loved public sharer of the Holocaust, found herself. Even as a child who couldn't have articulated it, I knew that no matter how much satisfaction sharing her story may have given her, the truth was that my grandmother would live with the demons and the memories of the past—as well as the problems of the present—forever. She would live with strife between herself and her only child, my mother, forever. She would live as someone who lost all but one member of her entire family, forever. I knew that no matter how loved she was by these audiences, there was a lot going on "behind the scenes" that was hard to swallow for anyone, even the strongest and most pragmatic of people. No amount of accolades and clapping audiences would change the past or bring her murdered family back or change her relationship with her daughter.

‡

I was as wanted, as welcomed and as treasured as a child could be and then some. For my grandparents, I was like a prize. A sign. A living, breathing representation that they had survived and that despite losing so very much, they had in the end, won. I knew all of this because they told me. I knew from the beginning how "special" and "different" I was.

From the beginning of any memory I have, I was at Bubby's apartment. Every picture of my first year of life was in her living room or her kitchen or—everyone's favorite—in my playpen with bare butt on her balcony (she lived on an upper floor of a high-rise—not the safest location, but whatever…). She was holding me; she was watching me; she was swinging me; she was feeding me. Every item of clothing seemed to have been handmade by her for me. Every spoonful of food came from her kitchen. Her friends were in and out of the apartment, all of them survivors, all speaking in Yiddish. They dreamed of their own grandchildren, who in most cases would come, but for the time being, Bubby was one of the first with one of these prizes of her very own.

Where were my parents? Dad was at work, building what would be a successful career. He worked a lot and was quickly becoming a well-known top attorney and real estate developer in DC. My grandparents were as proud of my dad as if he were their own son. He represented part of the dream, too: a successful Jewish son-in-law who'd graduated from Harvard Law School (did I mention the full scholarship?) and totally focused on his career as a way of taking care of his wife and new child. Mom's whereabouts are less clear. Physically, she may have been around, but emotionally, I believe she'd already begun checking out in some ways. She had very complicated and mixed feelings about me. She was proud of me and I know she loved me. But she also envied me and wished she had been born into my life instead of her own. How do I know this? Because she told me on many occasions, in different ways, over many years. So it made sense on several levels to hand me off to Bubby. And Bubby was a very willing participant, so everyone was better off.

The grandparent/grandchild relationship is traditionally a very special one. Given certain circumstances, such as the age and geographical proximity of the grandparent, it has all the ingredients for something that in some ways supersedes the parent/child relationship. All the time and patience and calm that Bubby didn't have in the 1950s and '60s for her own daughter, she had for her granddaughter—and then some. For years, before my sister came along, while Zeidy was at work and while my parents were doing their thing, it was just Bubby and me. Bubby was in her late fifties when I was born, still young, always healthy and utterly devoted. And I was a child, a heat-seeking missile for full attention and unconditional love. It was a "perfect storm" in which our relationship could be born, and it set the stage for nearly four decades of the most important relationship of my life.

As I got older, Bubby would tell me stories of just how brilliant and wonderful and beautiful I was as a baby, and later as a toddler, and then a small child. *"Alkele, you were nine months old, and I walked in with you to the lobby of my building. One of the ladies had a bag from Garfinkel's* [a popular local department store], *and you went right up to it, pointing and reading the name out loud."* I didn't pay a ton of mind to this story, which she told me countless times over the years, but the message was clear: *You are the smartest person in the room. Everyone should know how smart and clever you are.* (As an adult and a mother myself, I find it very hard to believe that at nine months old—*nine months old!*—I was reading words from shopping bags, out loud and for an audience, but I took the story at its face value for years and never would've thought to question it as a young child.)

Aftermath

Another story she'd tell, which I believe represented a combination of several similar stories, was how a group of her lady friends—all of them survivors, as were all of her friends in those years—were sitting in Bubby's living room, in a circle of sorts, all knitting or crocheting and chatting amongst themselves. I'd toddle in, perhaps taking a break from my favorite "office" game I played for hours on end at Bubby's, using all of her many office supplies, and all action would stop. With her usual dramatic flair in high gear, the way Bubby told the story, I imagined the knitting needles dropping to the floor and the ladies' faces freezing on the spot.

They'd all look at me adoringly, in awe, and then back at Bubby.

"*Goldeh,*" they'd say in Yiddish, using a word loosely translated to "golden" or something like "golden child." They'd all repeat the word, nodding in agreement that this child was indeed golden and special.

‡

These were the messages I grew up with: *You are special. You are different. We didn't get our chance, but you have yours, and you have everything you need to be the best, the first, the most.* It seemed like a positive and motivating message at the time and maybe today, to some it would still seem so. And in many ways, it was. Of course, this was how they— my grandparents, mostly, and my mom, too—knew how to love. They'd lost everything and now, in me, they saw a new chance, the best chance. I represented to them redemption. Hope. Opportunity.

When their daughter was born in 1947, they'd been in a refugee camp, for heaven's sake. They didn't have the means (or the time or the money or the will, for that matter) to demonstrate love, to shower her with affection (or much of anything) or in all likelihood, to focus on her emotions and needs in any significant way. After they moved to America, they were working day and night, adjusting to life in a whole new world. Their one child was left to her own devices in many cases, being raised by parents who likely had not even begun to process the tragedy they'd lived through just a few years earlier.

I was their second chance, maybe their last chance. When I was born in 1971, their survival was a story now decades old, not the fresh, open wound it had been in 1947 when my mom was born. From their perspective, I was pure potential and possibility. From mine, I was the object of all attention and didn't know there was any other way. As I grew up, though, with all of those lessons about being perfect now internalized and part of me, I never really knew that it was OK to not be perfect, or even that it wasn't really possible to be perfect. I took what they taught me to an extreme, because I knew no other way. I *had* to be the best, or I was the worst. I judged everyone around me by these same impossible standards and they, like me in most cases, never measured up.

Aftermath

‡

When I was five years old, and my mother told me I was going to have a new brother or sister before I was six, I was absolutely horrified. It felt like a betrayal, actually. *Why would they ever need to have a baby? Wasn't I enough? Weren't we doing great with just me?* My parents, and my dad in particular, did a great job of explaining how a new brother or sister would increase the love in our family, and how he or she would look up to me as their older sister, but I wasn't seeing it their way. (For those of you keeping score, I ended up accepting my sister, Erica, right off the bat, and we were always—and remain—very close.)

Later, as I got older, I tried in some ways to shrink back from the "perfect" and "best labels." While both Mom and Bubby were outspoken people, often commanding (demanding?) attention in a room or among people, I began to want to be on the sidelines and not have any eyes or ears focused on watching me or hearing what I had to say. Perhaps I didn't need the validation or attention of a crowd that they both needed. What they gained energy and drive from completely drained me. To this day, I need double or maybe even triple the "alone time" to the "people time" I have. If I feel someone is scrutinizing me or overly focused on me, I feel uncomfortable, thinking of how they may see how "not-perfect" I really am. When my own daughter was in her early teenage years, I would tell her over and over that people in her middle school were so wrapped up in themselves that they weren't even paying attention to what she was wearing or how she looked. We teach what we need to learn, and this was something I probably needed far more than she did. (She lost interest after the first "life lesson" or two.)

I now know, as a mom of two young adults, that building one's kids up to the sky is not actually the opposite of tearing them down. While most parents who over-praise their kids do so because they love them dearly, I now see there are inherent dangers to this approach. No one is always "the best" or "the smartest." No one can accomplish whatever they want just because they are good or smart or loved. Kids don't necessarily deserve trophies just because they showed up and played every game. (OK, that is a whole other discussion....) Telling them that they are the greatest, and then having them discover they aren't can be devastating. Rejection is inevitable, and it is not a commentary on our character or our potential. To this day, despite my many accomplishments and achievements, I feel they haven't been enough; I've fallen short; I've missed the boat in too many cases and so much more.

‡

1976

I WAS IN KINDERGARTEN, AND WE WOULD BE PLAYING OR BE involved in an activity until the teacher called for all of us to stop what we were doing and gather round in the circle area. I don't remember how it started, but somehow

Aftermath

I became, at some point, The One Everyone Wanted To Sit Next To. I didn't want that. I wasn't looking for a big posse. I was looking to blend in and not have so much attention paid to me. I wanted to sit where I wanted to sit and not cause a ruckus, and not command any attention, not from the teacher or from my friends. I wanted to be like everyone else.

So the teacher would signal that it was time to stop whatever we were doing, and as we made our way in a frenzied mass to the circle area, I'd do my best to just look straight ahead without making any eye contact and sit right down in place, continuing to look neither right nor left. The moment I would put bottom to floor, a bunch of kids would push and run to sit next to me. I didn't like that commotion, so I would get back up and attempt to move to another part of the circle to just sit alone without all these people around me. I knew the teacher didn't like the sitting-down-and-then-getting-up-again-to-sit-somewhere-else routine, so I tried to be discreet.

I just wanted to be left alone. To be seen less. Most people wanted more; I wanted less.

Instead, I ended up being singled out more as the teacher would mention me—and my indiscretion—by name.

"Allie," she would say, "Pick a spot and sit there. Do not move around and switch once you have sat down. Do you understand that?"

Yes, of course, I understood that. I understood everything, even at five or six years old. I got the rules, and I was all about following them. But I couldn't control these other people. And even though they were my peers and friends, I wanted them to leave me alone. To move on to another new, favorite person. To not get me into trouble with the teacher. All I was trying to do was be invisible. And not piss anyone off. All of which ended up making me more visible and caused me to piss everyone off.

When you learn early on how powerful a position the center of attention can be, you either seek that out and embrace it, or you avoid it and shirk its glare at all costs. I did the latter, as I was learning quickly how uncomfortable I felt in the spotlight. After all, I got enough of that at home.

Most kids come to school and seek out attention from their peers because they just don't get enough at home. I got too much and sought out anonymity at school.

‡

My lifetime of pushing and feeling pushed led to a perfectionist, judgmental nature that was perpetually disappointed and dissatisfied, mostly with myself and often with others. I was diagnosed at age twenty with an autoimmune condition that affected my thyroid and to this day, I feel certain that this was a condition born of my incessant pushing and striving. My immune system, reflecting its owner, became overzealous and overreacting, going overboard to protect me and doing damage to the very body it was meant to protect in the process. It took two more decades to gain control over this process and realize why this was happening.

I have absolutely no ill will or regret over being brought up this way. I was loved, I was wanted, I was treasured and for all of this (and more), I was fortunate. This was the only way they knew how to do what they were doing. These were broken people expressing love in the most whole way they knew how. These were people who still, on some days, probably couldn't believe their great fortune that allowed them to even have a grandchild. These were people who somehow—and to this day, I don't know how—were able to see the horrors no one should have to see and then go on to live in "normal" society as "normal" people. These were people, in my mom's case, who didn't have the tools—emotional, practical, or otherwise—to be as productive and healthy as they might have been under different circumstances.

In 2009, when I was in the midst of a divorce and at the height of a period of examining, breaking down and rebuilding everything I'd believed up until that point, I began to read a lot of twelve-step-related literature. While there was no alcohol or drug addiction in my family, as I learned about many of the codependent tendencies that can be common in family members of addicts, something resonated deeply within me. Yes, my being a perfectionist and my needing to feel in control and my blocks around loving myself exactly as I was were not things that just magically appeared out of the ether. Making sense of who we are, learning we are not the only ones and putting names to the feelings and patterns (without becoming over-reliant on these names and labels) is part of the most validating and empowering process I have ever experienced.

During this same time, I came across the term, "Family Hero," as one of the ways in which kids—who then, of course, become adults—try to manage their families that allows them to exist and manage and hopefully thrive as best as they know how.

Aftermath

THIS IS THE CHILD WHO IS *"9 GOING ON 40."* THIS CHILD *takes over the parent role at a very young age, becoming very responsible and self-sufficient. They give the family self-worth because they look good on the outside. They are the good students, the sports stars, the prom queens. The parents look to this child to prove that they are good parents and good people.*

As an adult the Family Hero is rigid, controlling, and extremely judgmental (although perhaps very subtle about it) – of others and secretly of themselves. They achieve "success" on the outside and get lots of positive attention but are cut off from their inner emotional life, from their True Self. They are compulsive and driven as adults because deep inside they feel inadequate and insecure.

The family hero, because of their "success" in conforming to dysfunctional cultural definitions of what constitutes doing life "right," is often the child in the family who as an adult has the hardest time even admitting that there is anything within themselves that needs to be healed.
~ Source: joy2meu.com

‡

I should say, "thank you" to Ashley Judd, for it was her amazing book, *All That Is Bitter and Sweet,* that first introduced me to these designations: the Family Hero or Responsible Child, the Scapegoat or Acting Out Child, the Caretaker or Placater/Mascot and the Lost Child or Adjuster. While I do not personally know Ashley, and she has no clue I exist, I now consider her a kindred spirit and will never cease being grateful to her for educating me about something that healed and changed my life in enormous ways.

While all of this is likely the topic of a whole other book, I can say that being introduced to the idea of the "Family Hero" was like being introduced to my own self. It's as if I had a condition or disease all along, but I didn't know it was a disease or condition, or that anyone outside of me had it, too. Imagine the surprise, then denial, then validation I felt when I learned that I was not the only family hero in the world. (Ironically, part of being the person in this role is believing that no one else can do what you do, that you "must" do certain things, save everyone, fix everything, so it makes perfect sense that as someone who so personified this role that I felt I was the only one.)

‡

As time went on, after Mom died and as Bubby got older, it fell to me to take on a lot of the "stuff" of Bubby's everyday life. I would joke that my family caregiving as a member of the "sandwich generation" took place a few decades early, as I was only in my thirties at the time. While I was an organized and responsive caregiver, and while I did what was needed (and then some), I don't feel I was actually a good one. As a perfectionist, I would get easily overwhelmed, usually by my own expectations and judgments, less so by anything Bubby did or said specifically. I took her projects and stresses on as my own, and I wasn't good at compartmentalizing, having perspective or when necessary, letting go.

One of the most frustrating and stressful duties related to taking care of Bubby's life had to do with the German government. Yes, there it was, decades later, still having power over our lives! Bubby received reparations in the form of two monthly checks in the mail from the German government. The amounts would vary based on the exchange rate with the German mark. One was considered like a pension, representing the time she "worked" for the German government while incarcerated in the ghetto. I always found this curious, ironic. But it was money, and as she was elderly with no other sources of income (except Social Security), it was welcome. The other payment was the check for reparations, the "We are sorry for what we did, killing your family and imprisoning and torturing and starving you and all" money. Every year, Bubby had to go through a rigorous process to be re-approved for the payments. It was more than a simple form with name and contact information. She had to prove who she was, that she was still alive and go through all sorts of hoops to get the checks for one more year. I felt these people had a lot of nerve doing what they did to millions of people and then demanding that the survivors, most by that time elderly, have the burden of proof on them. The times I had to deal with them directly to ask questions or make clarifications were excruciating. I may have thought I was a person who was very exact, even OCD in some areas, but I had nothing on these German bureaucrats.

In addition to all of this, Bubby was trying to have some of her home care, which she needed to a small extent starting around 2003 or 2004 and increasing over the few years until she died, paid for by the German government, as well. To have this covered, she had to prove that the incapacitation was caused, at least in part, by the depression and other lasting mental anguish brought on by the Germans' treatment of her during the Holocaust. Again, more hoops. More paperwork. More arguing and proving and begging. On more than one occasion, I came very close to giving these Germans a real piece of my mind. I wasn't used to a situation like this, being wronged (egregiously, to say the least) and then still having to play nice to the aggressors because they still had some form of control over you. A victim who still had to kowtow to the party that made them a victim in the first place. It was mind-blowing. Also, when dealing with the Germans, apparently there was a very specific way one had to act and present the information. It was all very black and white, with no emotions despite the massive emotional history there. Bubby was pretty good at it; I was terrible at it.

Truth be told, I hated what she had to do, and I hated

having to start doing it for her. I hated having to pretend to respect the system or even to understand it. I hated that she still had to ask them for permission of any kind, and that I now had to do this for her. Mom never did any of it; why did everything fall on me?

All of Bubby's communications with the German government in Saarburg, Germany or with its consulate in Washington, DC (and later, after she moved to Florida, in Miami) was conducted by handwritten letter or in less of the cases, phone. Email was not an option in the early days, so she'd wait for weeks (sometimes longer) for a reply.

PAULA DASH
Bethesda, MD 20817

[translated from the German]

Dept. of Reparation
In Saarburg Herkingstr. 37
54439 Saarburg

July 10

Dear Sir,

I am very sad; to begin with, it is already the 10th of July and I have not yet received my pension check.

Then, when you answered my concerns regarding my account, you even informed me that I should have been receiving an additional [amount of money} starting in November. However, I received nothing, neither my pension nor my subsidy.

Please look into what may have happened. I am impatiently waiting for your response.

With kind regards,

Frau Paula Dash

~ One of many letters handwritten, in Bubby's distinctive European script, asking about money but really begging for understanding and compassion.

Aftermath

‡

The same week Bubby died, she received a monthly check from Germany. Without a second thought, I deposited it in her account, knowing full well that she'd have the same bills that month even though it was her last month. Almost immediately, I received a letter from the Germans informing me that I'd committed fraud and needed to return the money without delay. I felt such shame! *Fraud? Me?* And such anger, too. *Really? You're concerned with this one last check that will be used to pay her electric bill? You take your sweet time answering an old lady's handwritten letters asking for clarification or information, but when she dies and is no longer due any money from you, boy, are you on the case fast!* They managed to take back the money themselves from her account, but not before putting all sorts of "warnings" and "alerts" on the account, signaling it as possibly fraudulent. They started to send me letter after letter (again, demonstrating their wonderful industriousness, they were able to get my name from the bank account, as Bubby's account listed me as the joint owner, since I was managing all of her bills and other administrative responsibilities).

I don't remember the exact words, but I wrote those formal jerks a scathing letter, including something along the lines of: *Because of you, we have no family. You sent them all to death. Because of you, my mom eventually committed suicide. Do you really want to keep pursuing this matter, accusing honest people of fraud over a few hundred dollars?*—of which, again, they'd taken back already.

Hey, I was stressed out and my Bubby had just died. I'm OK with how I responded, so it's cool.

Plus, I never heard from them again.

Chapter 6

THE SADDEST THING IN LIFE
IS WASTED TALENT

Much has been written, studied and reported on the children of Holocaust survivors, the so-called Second Generation. Many in this generation have been significantly and as often as not, negatively, affected by their parents' experiences and subsequent parenting.

And understandably so. They grew up in the aftermath of something so incomprehensible, so evil, yet so a part of all that they were and all that they lived. Even now, I can't imagine what it was like: my grandparents as new immigrants to the United States. They literally had nothing—no family, no material possessions, just each other and whatever they wore on their backs or carried in their hands. My mother grew up not understanding, yet understanding everything. They spoke Yiddish. They had precious few relatives (from my grandmother's side, only one brother survived). And try as she might, my grandmother was unable to carry any more babies to term.

My mother grew up full of anger, resentment, regret and constant unhappiness. She longed for a brother or sister with whom she could share the burden (how she viewed it) of having parents with these experiences. She longed to be like the more well-off members of the community. She often told a story about a doll she treasured until another girl approached her in the street and announced that the doll had, in fact, been hers until her mom donated it to a charity for poor people with no toys.

My mom, Lily Dash Blankstein, was not like the other moms. I knew that from early on. I think everyone knew that. She'd yearned for what she now had, but it wasn't what she wanted. She was a wife and a mother, a well-to-do suburban housewife who wanted to do and be something. She knew more than most people, and she wanted you to know that she knew more, that she was smarter. (I have these tendencies, too, and am working on better understanding them and myself.) She threw great parties and spared no expense. When we went on a family vacation, she insisted on not only the best hotel, but the best suite in the hotel. I wouldn't say she had us living beyond our means, because the means were there, but it shouldn't have been spent on catering and top-of-the-line vacations. But my dad gave her free rein, likely because of the alternative—a confrontation with her, which started at 8.5 on a scale of 1–10 and always ended somewhere around 16.

Aftermath

Mom was smart. Like scary smart. Like smartest-person-in-the-room smart (except for maybe my dad). And she wanted you to know it. On our many trips to New York City, my sister and I would dread every time we got into a taxi, knowing any moment Mom would start up a conversation with the driver that invariably began with a guessing game about the origin of his accent. She'd nail it on the first or second try, and the more obscure the country, the more impressed the driver would be. This would lead to an animated conversation in which my mom demonstrated to the driver just how much she knew about his home country, resulting in two people feeling fantastic about themselves: my mom about her knowledge of a country most of her peers had probably not heard of and the driver about his homeland, proud of its "high profile" among Americans. Without a doubt, Mom would've loved Uber.

She was funny and sharp, and her humor could be sarcastic and clever, even biting at times. If you weren't super-quick and whip-smart, you might not "get" her, but you'd still be impressed and likely intrigued. You had to be on your toes around my mom and lucky for her, there were people who enjoyed that sort of "always-on" wittiness and banter. As an adult, I think that dynamic would be quite tiring and draining for me, and perhaps that is a direct result of being a close observer—perhaps the closest—for all the early years of my life.

‡

The saddest thing in life is wasted talent,
and the choices that you make
will shape your life forever.

~ A Bronx Tale

That was my mom's favorite line from a favorite movie. It was a favorite movie because it spoke to her, deeply, about love and connection and community, but it did not actually touch upon her own history, so it was safe. (Italians in the Bronx were unthreatening to Jews of the Holocaust…in her mind.) It was a favorite line because she knew all about wasted talent. About potential that never amounted to more. About a life lived but never really *lived.*

That's her story, I thought. Her journey was one of sadness and sorrow, of good things never realized and of an inability to make sense of or be at peace with any of it. I've worked hard to make sure my story is different. That I could make peace with the past, all the while honoring it and her. For many years, I hated my mom's story. I was threatened by it. Scared, perhaps, at how easily it could've been mine.

The last conversation my mom and I had in person took place in February of 1998, two months before she was gone. This ended up being the last time I saw her alive. What she told me didn't resonate much at the time, but was to stay with me forever. It was to inspire much of my future writing, and it was to pop itself into my head at the strangest times. It was simple, yet profound. It was about coping and living, surviving and pushing.

"We only have a finite amount of energy we can push and push and push. Unless we have ways of replenishing, once we use it up, it's gone. And then we might have nothing left for what might have really mattered. I know because I wasted all of mine. I have nothing left. I don't want that to happen to you."

This is what she told me.

Wasted talent.

Spent energy.

Pushing. People. Energy. Life.

Potential.

Gone.

Hair

Mom wanted to be noticed, to be seen. And perhaps the most outward visual manifestation of that desire was her hair.

Oh, her hair.

Even now, years after she died and decades after we were kids, people still talk—in awe and with great reverence—about Mom's hair. My mom was all about her hair. It was—quite literally—her "crowning glory." It was almost not human: the thickness, the lushness, the length, the weight. It was like a softer and even thicker version of a horse's mane. The color was a shiny golden, enhanced by the best salon services money could buy.

But salon aside, it was the kind of hair that even the best professionals couldn't just create. It was something you were born with (or not). And something very few people are born with. I don't know where it came from, as neither Bubby nor Zeidy had it.

When I was growing up, my mom's hair was with me everywhere. It was almost like another, more important, more demanding member of my family. It came first. Her hair came first. Before, well, most anything else. I spent many, many... (Did I say

MANY?) Saturdays at one salon or another as my mom had her hair done. Washed, blown out, braided in the thickest, most gravity- and reality-defying French braid ever known to womankind.

I'd sit in that salon for two, three, four, five hours. Every Saturday. With nothing to do. As was the case in the regular visits to the therapist, I didn't have any handheld devices, games, cell phones, iPods or any entertainment that my kids wouldn't dare leave home without. I had no way to pass the time, yet the time passed. Not quickly or easily, but it passed. Sometimes, my mom wasn't happy with the braid. Or the bangs. Or the color. So she might have demanded that it be redone, or rebraided or retrimmed. And I'd sit there for an hour more.

To this day, as I've shared, I go out of my way to never take my own kids, now teenagers, on my errands with me. Not the longer events like a haircut or pedicure, not even on a quick grocery store run. From the time they were babies, I have made sure that I take care of my own personal business or even the business of the family (shopping, drycleaners, bank, etc.) on my "own" time. I cannot recall even one instance in nearly two decades of parenting in which I dragged one or both kids along on a boring errand, let alone forcing them to endure hours on end in a salon on a Saturday afternoon.

Also in direct reaction to Mom's high "mainte-
nance-ness" when it came to her looks and grooming,
I go out of my way to be as low-maintenance as I
can possibly be. To an extreme, sometimes. I down-
play my hair. I under-do my makeup. I can get ready
quickly. I don't need someone to do my hair. I don't
do salons. I make sure everyone knows how natural
and simple I can really be.

As I was growing up, it all seemed normal. And
natural. My mom spent her days, or at least her Saturdays, in the salon. And that's where I belonged on
Saturdays. I didn't think much of it, and I always
liked the part where I got to have a toasted bagel
dripping with real butter from the place across the
street. That was something I never got at home, and
it brought me comfort on those long afternoons (can
you say, "emotional eating"?). Sometimes, one of the
assistants or maybe the hairdresser's daughter would
do my hair. It always looked beautiful, maybe styled
into two, French-braided pigtails or blown straight
out. I was complimented by everyone. But I didn't
care about the compliments; they didn't make me feel
good. In fact, they scared me. Because the better my
hair looked and the more people who noticed, the
more I would be like my mom.

‡

Aftermath

At the other end of the hair spectrum was Bubby's story. While my present-day life featured Mom's hair as a major player, so did the Holocaust side of my life feature Bubby's hair, or more to the point, her hair story, as a major player.

‡

This was in August. Twenty-first of August. I told you, the ghetto. We had to leave the ghetto. And we took showers and then they shaved our hair. We didn't recognize each other. And then we got, so to speak, we got clothes. They gave us dresses from dead people. I got a big dress, a long dress. I could hardly walk in it. And then we had to, we had to run to the barracks barefoot on the gravel. They put us in the barracks. There were bunk beds, three tiers, with raw wood. Plenty of splinters. Fourteen girls in one bunk bed.

So we were several days in this atmosphere in Auschwitz. And then transports kept on coming and coming and coming and they didn't have a place for us in the barracks. So they put us out one day in the field, a big, big field, naked. We were sitting there all day and all night. And we were waiting till the next morning to be gassed. Going to the crematorium.

‡

It goes without saying that the enormity of the mixed messages I was receiving could make a person's head spin.

But there was no one in my life, though well-meaning and loving in their own way they all were, who sat me down to explain that these extremes were not the reality of what I should be modeling after, nor were they part of a future I would fashion for myself. I'd go to friends' houses and see that no one's hair, nor the parents, nor the kids (or the grandparents) took center stage; in fact, they took no stage. I noticed the differences in families, but there wasn't anything I could do with that information. It wasn't something I could take home with me and apply to my own situation.

When we went on our extravagant family vacations, whether to the South of France or England or Cannes or Beverly Hills, we'd all be prisoners of my mom and her hair. Our days would not even start until one or two in the afternoon. There was no such thing as an early (or even a regular) morning start in my family. Because Mom had to do her hair. And "doing her hair" meant hours of rollers and round brushes and hairspray, and of pulling and teasing and pulling again.

In those hours between, say, 9:00 a.m. and 1:00 p.m. or 2:00 p.m., when we would finally venture out of a hotel room or a condo we were renting, or wherever we were staying, there would, inevitably, be a fight. A verbal knockdown, blowout kind of fight. The kind that I only learned years later was not normal or in any way productive in its ferocity or intensity. The fight was usually between my mom and me or my mom and my dad. Mom was always involved. When

Aftermath

Bubby and Zeidy were on the vacation with us, they were involved, too, almost always as the objects of Mom's wrath. Those fights were in Yiddish and took on a different tone and approach than the fights between Mom and Dad. All of these fights directly reflected, but in a more amplified version, the Friday night Shabbat (the Jewish Sabbath) dinner blowouts at home. These arguments blend together in my memory, as they were the norm at home or away on vacation. They almost never did not happen. I don't remember a fight-free or low-maintenance-hair vacation ever.

Once, as we waited in the fancy sitting room of one of the fancy suites we were staying in somewhere, my dad, in a rare moment of emotional nakedness that he rarely engaged in, told me in a quiet but very firm voice,

"Allie, when you grow up, don't focus on your looks. Don't waste your time worrying about your hair or your makeup. It takes too much time, and you'll never be happy from that.

"Enjoy yourself and don't get wrapped up in what you look like, like your Mom. It will only lead to unhappiness. Your mom spends hours and hours on herself and still isn't happy. I know you will be different."

I was in my early teens when he told me this. He was right, and I never forgot his advice. Of course, as is more common than not with a teenage girl, my goal was to be everything exactly as my mom was not. And as was common with me and my black-or-white approach, I took this vow to the extreme. The next twenty-plus years became a constant, exhausting, all-consuming quest to be, do and live as the antithesis of my mom. And by being the antithesis of my mom, I ended up bringing myself closer and closer to Bubby, who, in my mind (and because of the dynamics of the family, and the fighting), was the opposite of Mom. Brave, bold, beautiful in an inner-fire and lasting sort of way. Letting her actions speak for themselves. This was a kind of strength that my mother, try as she might, couldn't actually compete with. You had it or you didn't, and Bubby did.

‡

Later in her life, toward the end, Mom became exhausted. She couldn't keep trying so hard to prove whatever she was trying to prove. She wasn't her mom and she never would be. She'd pushed my dad away, lost him and now wanted him back, despite having been the one to leave in the first place. She became softer and more approachable. She even gave me some mom-like lessons that she'd never been very good at or fond of. The last conversation we had together in person was on the couch in my family home on Sorrel Avenue in Potomac, Maryland. It was clear she was on a downward slide. She was very low. She rarely moved from the couch, and her life was mostly confined to the couch, the coffee table, the television (on mute) and the boom box (on Howard Stern or G. Gordon Liddy, depending on the time of day, at full blast). To some extent, she let Bubby mother her a bit, but Bubby, who was already in her eighties, needed to protect herself and had no one else to take care of her.

In that last conversation, I tried to tell her how much she had to live for and how much joy she would get from Daniel, her first grandchild, born just two months earlier. I don't know if she was really hearing what I was saying; likely, she was too far gone at that point to absorb any of it. By that time, she wasn't able to do any of the basic activities of daily life, such as sorting through the mail (I later found piles and piles of unopened mail) or filling up the car with gas.

"You have so much to live for," I said to her, perhaps as much to myself. I was in the throes of what was likely post-partum depression, as well. *"You have a new grandchild; you have everything you need to be happy. There is so much joy in the most simple things in life. Stop focusing on what went wrong and look at all you already have."*

She didn't even answer me. It was too hard on her, realizing what she'd lost, what she could never regain, what she never had in the first place. She knew Dad was gone to her, and while she had never been blissfully happy with him, she saw in him all the dreams and hopes she'd once had now permanently gone. He had been the one who was meant to rescue her from a life of Holocaust survivors, from a childhood of disappointment and never enough, from her own self. Of course, he had not done any of these things, nor would he have been able to, and she'd never forced herself to rescue her own self. Now, at this point, she could barely get up from the sofa to use the bathroom, let alone become self-aware and proactive enough to begin to truly heal from all the pain she'd lived with literally since the day she was born.

Just two months later, Bubby would find Mom dead on the couch in that same family room.

‡

My mom had killed herself. I was someone whose mother had killed herself.

Here's my thinking on this: Cancer is awful but acceptable. Same for car accidents. Even freak accidents. But suicide? Not so much. No one wants to hear about suicide. It is too raw, too uncomfortable. Suicide details are swept under the rug and ignored at all costs.

As I learned again and again over the years, suicide was, to say the least, a conversation killer. So quickly, instantly, the approach became: avoid talking about suicide at all costs. Pretend. Change the story. Add innocent details. No need to lie, of course. Just massage the truth. But whatever happens, don't mention suicide! But I saw the pills. The wine. The papers with scribbled, chicken-scratched notes. I saw that she lived all day and slept (sort of) all night on the family room sofa. I saw how she had CNN or another all-news TV channel on, muted, all day and all night. And talk radio blasting all day and maybe all night, too.

I saw the piles of mail, unopened. The messages waiting

to be listened to, responded to, on the answering machine. The unused rooms in the huge, echoing house. The permanent indentation of her body on the couch that had become her home base. But beyond all of those signs, all of those unanswered cries for help, I had seen something that above all else should have told me just how done my mom was. How done she was with life, with her pursuit of something—anything.

I saw that she had already given up. At some point in that last year, she'd had to cut her hair. It started to look like, well, an average person's hair. It looked like it could belong to anyone else. She'd cut it drastically (to her shoulders or above). The color was frosty and overdone, not unlike many blonde women who went too far with the blonde. It was drab and had lost all of its life. It needed a lot more than the salon treatment. Her hair looked like it belonged to someone else. Someone at whom you'd never look twice on the street or in the mall. Someone whose hair just *was*, no more, no less. Irrational or not, my belief remains that I should have realized, when my mom stopped caring about her hair, the dire straits she was in. Her hair was not worthy of a double-take, and the double-take (and triple-take, and quadruple-take) was precisely what my mom had lived for. And now, it had become average at best.

But I had my own stuff going on. I was overwhelmed and stopped in my tracks by what I now know was postpartum depression following the birth of my first child two months before. I was, on so many levels, a mess. I wasn't in a place to help myself, let alone my mom. I saw much of what was happening and knew what could happen, but I didn't feel that I had the power or the emotional means to help or change. I lived through years of the guilt and the "what ifs." They are all part of my story, but not the most productive or instructive part. Part of my lesson, one of the great lessons of my life and one that I believe bears repeating, is that we cannot change or control everything. In fact, we can't change or control a whole heck of a lot.

‡

My mom longed to shine her light. She longed to take "center stage." She longed to shine but was unable (or unwilling) to let go of lots of darkness and other light-blockers. She didn't want to be wasted talent like the warning story in *A Bronx Tale*. We all missed out on who-even-knows-what-great-things because she didn't get herself together. But that doesn't mean her life was in vain. That doesn't mean she was nameless. Maybe her role was to form a bridge, a bridge between the survivors who needed something real and beautiful onto which to stake their hopes and dreams, something to keep them going. Something that would lead to a new generation and eventually, to my sister and me. Maybe her role, as painful and fleeting as it was, was to be that middle person. Maybe she knew it, and she resented it. She wanted more than the middle. She didn't think she could lead or shine from that middle. She could, and she did, but it wasn't right or enough or what she wanted. She wasn't the speaker upon whom admiration and attention were showered. How could she be? She did not survive the camps, yet she was still as much a victim of their aftermath as anyone else. Nor was she the cherished and treasured grandchild, the one who offered all hopes of redemption, all chances to make things right and better. She "missed out" on this adoration and attention. She didn't have a grandmother to shower her in that kind of love. No wonder she felt wronged and short-changed…she *was* wronged and short-changed.

But so are many people in life. And as far as being wronged goes, she sure had every gift and comfort afforded to her so that she could right those wrongs and live differently and better. But she didn't use them to her advantage. You could say she wasted them. Preferred the story of what was dead and gone to the story of what could be. That is a story that never has a happy ending. And so she lived a life cut all too short and defined at each step of the way by tragedy and resentment and loss. In a sense, she created a whole new chapter that mirrored its predecessor in all the wrong ways. Except that this time, she had control and power. She had the freedom to break the cycle and change her life. And she did not take those reins. She did not become who she very well could have been. It was a tragedy of a wholly different kind, but a tragedy nonetheless.

And so we went on without Mom. In some ways, life was smoother. It was less about what had gone wrong in the past and what was wrong with the past. It became more about now and the future. We started to look forward more. Bubby was no longer scared of being verbally attacked and emotionally challenged by her daughter. I was amazed at how calm and easy being together as a family became. But we were a tiny little bunch, with holes. Nothing ever took away the hole that Mom being gone made in our lives. Our bridge was gone. Sure, there were other ways of bringing it all together—and we were smart; we could figure it out—but our most natural choice never panned out.

‡

SANDY

When I was sixteen, I met up at the mall food court with my mom's good friend, Sandy. Sandy, too, was a child of Holocaust survivors, and she was an accomplished historian and teacher. I was only a teenager, but I knew full well that Sandy had her stuff together in a way that Mom did not, maybe could not. On this particular occasion, Sandy had been dispatched to the mall by my mom to talk to me and help bring about some peace during a particularly contentious period in our mother/daughter relationship.

Sandy told me about her own experience growing up, and in language I could understand, explained just how isolating and difficult it could be growing up as the child of survivors. They were immigrants, but not "regular" immigrants. They were Jews, but not "regular" American Jews.

Aftermath

"I understood your mom; that's why we became friends," she told me. No one had ever put it in those terms to me before. As a teenager, the last thing that I cared about was understanding my parents or their motivations. Heck, I barely looked at them as real people separate of me or my life. "Our own parents were unable to parent us in any sort of normal way. They were traumatized, and they passed that trauma on to us. It wasn't a bad childhood, but it was in no way easy or anything like yours. That's what we were dealt, and I have spent my life trying to break that cycle now with my own kids."

I did understand Sandy. But I knew in my heart that while she had vowed to break the cycle and was doing that very thing in her own life, my mom had not vowed any such thing. Not that she didn't want to break the cycle; surely she did. But she wasn't present enough in reality to recognize that such a thing could be done, nor was she equipped to actually break the cycle. While Sandy was a strong and capable woman, my mom was too torn down by her anger and resentment to take on and carry out something as potentially overwhelming or difficult.

"Your Mom loves you, and she is doing the best she can do, Allie," Sandy said. I wondered, as I had times before, why my mom didn't have herself together. Was it really that hard? She was a relatively wealthy woman. She was healthy and compared to the parents of most of my friends, she was young. She was whip-smart, and she was beautiful. She had all the ingredients she needed to do anything she wanted in life.

I think an ordinary life scared the hell out of my mom. It wasn't enough. It wouldn't ever be enough. She needed a spotlight or a stage. Something that would showcase her talents and smarts to the world. Maybe she needed the adoration and attention of many to make up for the lack from her parents that she felt she received growing up. The usual tasks of every day, such as writing a check or mailing a letter or changing a light bulb were things that I never saw Mom do. She was overwhelmed by these little things and focused instead on expectations that were ultimately not only unmet, but impossible to start with.

‡

When Mom died in 1998, I think she broke the cycle in the only way she knew how. It was a permanent and lasting way, for sure. I remembered my food court talk with Sandy, and I knew that was the best that Mom could have done with what she had at that time. It wasn't the positive and productive way that Sandy had broken it, but it was broken nonetheless. Now it was my turn to heal and grow in a more healthy and lasting way.

Was it before her time, out of sequence in the natural order of things? Yes, of course it was. Had she been what I wanted, what I needed, as a daughter? No, she hadn't been. Was it enough for me as a daughter? No, it wasn't. But I vowed I wouldn't spend my life with resentment and anger for the trauma that came before me and that, somehow, managed to still live and breathe in the present day.

From there, we moved forward, because that is what Bubby taught us to do. Well, not taught. Showed. That's what she showed us in the way she lived. And now we had a new generation: my first child, Daniel, and less than two years later, my daughter, Maya. I was determined the stories they got about our family history were something to be proud of and not something to have to live under. Unlike their grandmother Lily, who'd suffered so mightily under the weight of this burden, my kids would have a different experience, a new story. I'd break the cycle my mom never could break herself. I knew it wouldn't be easy; if it were easy, it would've already been done, right? But I knew I had to do it. For all of our sakes. In honor of my mom, and in lieu of her, too. I vowed that my kids would know where they came from and how they got here. I'd see to it that they carried their legacy like the gift that it was.

Today, I love and appreciate my mom more than ever. More than that, I truly understand her. All that was good about her lives on, of this I am certain.

Bubby and Zeidy with their daughter, my mom, in the late 1940s.

Can you imagine surviving what they survived and living to see a grand-child born? Me, at five-months-old, with my grandparents in November 1971.

Aftermath

My Zeidy, front and center between the two women, leading a post-war Zionist parade ca. 1946.

The Activist

These photos show the rubble and all-around destruction in Germany toward the end of the war. This clean-up was the type of work that, while grueling, saved Bubby and the other women like her who were, by a miracle, plucked from certain death at Auschwitz.

Aftermath

This is the only surviving prewar photo of anyone from Bubby's family. This is a passport photo of her father, Aaron. As the war drew closer, he tried to get himself and his family out of Poland and to Palestine (Israel). He was too late and never able to leave, but his passport application and its accompanying photo survived. Bubby enlarged this photo and framed it, and it hung prominently in all of her homes for her entire life.

Bubby, in her first few years in America.

Me around four-years-old doing my favorite thing: Playing "office" at Bubby's. I would set up a "TV table" with all of my office supplies and keep myself occupied for hours doing transactions and organizing my workspace.

With their only child at her wedding, 1970.

Aftermath

This photo is a relatively recent find for me. It shows my parents and my grandparents at Mom and Dad's 1970 wedding. As of 2016, all four of these souls have passed on. I miss each one so very much. I hope so deeply that they are proud of me. There is something so pure and joyful about this photo. It now sits in my office where I can see it (and they can all watch over me) every day.

Zeidy taking a quick break at his Rodman's job.
The sweetest man you would ever meet.

At an exhibit on the Lodz Ghetto at the Yad Vashem museum in Jerusalem, Israel, I walked into a room where a video was playing and noticed my grandmother appearing in it! To this day, it blows my mind. The voiceover narration in the subtitle across the screen: "Whoever did not work was sent to his death." Bubby was a very skilled seamstress throughout her entire life, and I am certain her skills helped her survive as she did.

Mom and Bubby on a trip to Germany in 1991.

Bubby speaking at the UJA (United Jewish Appeal) headquarters in New York City where I worked in the mid-'90s.

At another speaking engagement, telling her story.

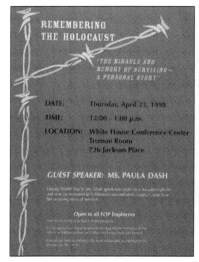
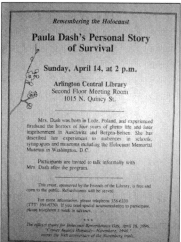

Speaking at the White House, 1998.

This jar sits in my office, where I am inspired by it every day. Bubby's note reads: "Fraction of the monument in Obernheide near Bremen [Germany]. One of the camps I was incarcerated." This is a gift that reminds me of where my cells have been and what was overcome so that I could be here today. Silly complaints and daily nonsense pale in comparison to what this piece of rock represents.

Aftermath

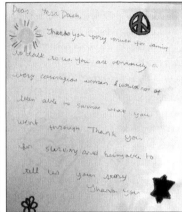

Thank you notes from teenagers who heard Bubby speak at various events.

Dear Misses Dash,
Thank you for coming to speak with us!
I thought your story about the holicast
was moving!
I will remember your story for as
long as I live!

Dear Mrs Dash,
Thank you very much for coming to our congregation
and sharing your story with us. I understand how
difficult and hard it must have been to relive
those horrible memories. I will never forget your
shocking story of the terrible memories of the
Holocaust. It took a lot of courage to stand
up in front of a group teenagers and tell your
stories. I promise I will always pass
on your story. Thank you again.

January 17, 1995

Dear Mrs. Dash,

Your story really touched me. It must be really hard to have been in your situation at that time. I know it is hard reading and watching about it but really experiencing it must be terrible.

I didn't really know much about the holocaust until I went to hebrew school and learned because my grandparent on one side were from Morroco and the other side from Ireland.

I also really appreciate you coming in and sharing with us your experience. Thank you very much

---

July 29, 2006

Mrs. Dash!

Thank you for your response to my letter. I'm very appreciative of your response. I tried to write you a letter last October, but it came back returned. I wrote it when I was 16, now I'm 17 I will be a Senior in highschool this fall.
I am happy that you will answer my questions.

I look forward to hearing from you again.

Aftermath

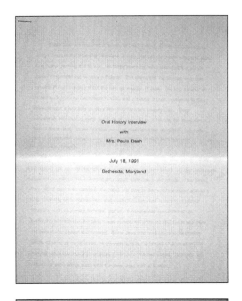

One of many student reports on Bubby.

School newspaper article on Bubby.

One of many articles about Bubby's experiences.

Frei und aufrecht zurückgekehrt

Ehemalige Zwangsarbeiterinnen gedachten in Stuhr der Leidenszeit

Stuhr (ujo). "Hier sind wir, frei und aufrecht stehen wir auf dem Platz, an dem wir als Sklaven gehalten worden sind." Die gedichtähnliche Ansprache der älteren Frau im Rathaus der Gemeinde Stuhr geriet ins Stocken bei der Erinnerung an die Vergangenheit, bei der Erinnerung an ihre Zeit in Stuhr. Denn sie gehört zu den 98 Frauen, die während des Nationalsozialismus als Zwangsarbeiterinnen hier gefangengehalten worden sind.

In Stuhr befand sich von 1944 bis 1945 die Außenkommandostelle Obernheide des Konzentrationslagers Neuengamme. 500 ungarische und 300 polnische Jüdinnen erlitten während dieser Zeit Demütigungen und Qualen, Hunger und Tod. Als die Frauen und ihre Angehörigen gestern wieder auf diesem denkwürdigen Platz standen, nun, da regte sich so manches, vergangenes Leid. Blumen und Blumenkränze wurden an dem 1988 errichteten Mahnmal niedergelegt, es wurden Gebete gesprochen und gesungen, aber es wurde auch gelacht, Fotokameras klickten und Filmkameras summten. Und diese Stimmung unterschied sich sichtlich von der aller vorherigen Besuche der Frauen.

Dr. Hartmut Müller, Leiter des Bremer Staatsarchivs, ist es zu verdanken, daß die "dunkle Vergangenheit" von Obernheide überhaupt ans Licht kam. Ihm fiel durch Zufall eine Akte in die Hand, die auf das Lager hinweist. Er recherchierte, befragte Augenzeugen, und es entstand das Buch "Die Frauen von Obernheide", das den Leidensweg der Frauen nachzeichnet.

1987 entschied der Stuhrer Gemeinderat, auf dem ehemaligen Lagerplatz ein Mahnmal zu errichten. Gemeindedirektor Hermann Rendigs gestern: "Die Gemeinde Stuhr möchte mit diesem Mahnmal ein Zeichen der Hoffnung setzen für eine Wiederannäherung zwischen Juden und Deutschen, wenn das überhaupt nach dem Holocaust noch denkbar ist." Lilly Maor, die die inzwischen in aller Welt lebenden Frauen zusamenbrachte, überreichte Bürgermeister Heinz-Wilhelm Schmidt ein Bild mit der innigen Bitte, daß die Stuhrerinnen und Stuhrer immer wieder an das Lager und an die Frauen von Obernheide erinnern möchte.

96 ehemalige Zwangsarbeiterinnen legten gestern am Mahnmal in Stuhr-Obernheide Kränze und Blumen nieder. Die Frauen waren 1944 und 1945 im KZ Obernheide inhaftiert. Foto: Gallmeier

German newspaper coverage of Bubby and her "girls" being honored in Bremen in 1991. Bubby is in the photo, left side, eight ladies back.

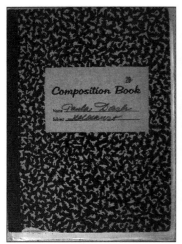
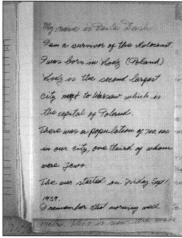

Let me tell you about this Composition Book. I think it was surgically attached to Bubby for decades. It went everywhere with her. It probably should have been the cover of this book. Her life story is contained within this notebook, and she shared it willingly and bravely with thousands over the years. A treasure I will keep with me until my last day on this Earth. I love how she filled out the front with "Holocaust" as the subject. On the right is the first page of her speech/story.

Health records for three new Americans: Mom, Zeidy, Bubby.

Aftermath

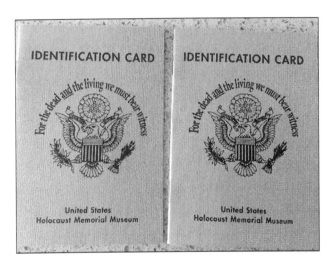

*Identification Cards from the U.S. Holocaust Museum in Washington, DC.
Many adults and teens from all over the world walked through the museum
"as" one of my grandparents. They were both so young in these photos.*

Name: Paula Garfinkel
Date of Birth: December 3, 1920
Place of Birth: Lodz, Poland

Paula was one of four children
born to a religious Jewish family
in Lodz, an industrial city with
a large Jewish population. As a
child, Paula attended public
schools and was tutored at home
in Jewish studies three times a
week. Her father owned a furniture store.

Please turn page at end of 4th floor.

Name: Shlomo Reich
Date of Birth: June 18, 1914
Place of Birth: Lodz, Poland

Shlomo was one of seven children
born in Lodz to the Reich family.
The Reichs were a religious Jewish
family, and Shlomo's Hasidic
father wore earlocks and a traditional fur hat. After public
school every day, Shlomo attended
the Ostrovtze Yeshiva, a rabbini-
cal academy where he studied
Jewish holy texts. Shlomo's
father owned a shoelace factory.

Please turn page at end of 4th floor.

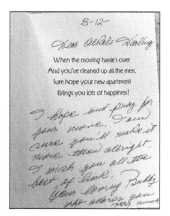

Congratulating me on my move to Florida, 1998. "I hope and pray for your move. I am sure you'll make it more than allright [sic]. I wish you all the best of luck. Your loving Bubby who adores you very much."

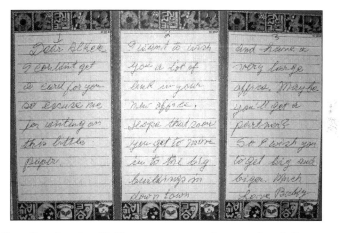

One of my favorites. Bubby wrote me notes, letters and cards for every occasion and milestone. This note was related to a new office: "Dear Alkele, I couldn't get a card for you so excuse me for writing on this little paper. I want to wish you a lot of luck in your new office. Hope that soon you get to move in to the big buildings in downtown and have a very large office. Maybe you'll get a partner? So I wish you to get big and biger [sic]. Much Love Bubby"

Aftermath

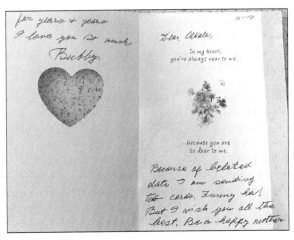

"Because of belated date I am sending two cards. Funny ha! But I wish you all the best. Be a happy mother for years and years. I love you so much Bubby."

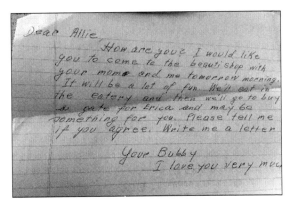

Dear Allie, How are you? I would like you to come to the beautishop [sic] with your mom and me tomorrow morning. It will be a lot of fun. We'll eat in the eatery and then we'll go to buy a gate for Erica and maybe something for you. Please tell me if you agree. Write me a letter.
Your Bubby
I love you very much"

Our family was included in a 1981 Washington Post story about Holocaust survivors and their families entitled, "Holocaust Heirs." This article coincided with the time that the second generation began developing its voice and coming into its own. Although I hated my itchy wool sweater with all of my heart, I adore this photo for many reasons.

Bubby and I at her last Passover, 2007.

Aftermath

My sister, Erica, and I with Bubby at her Bethesda, Maryland, apartment not long before she moved away to Florida. She loved dressing for a special occasion.

Always dressed to the nines.

Another favorite I will keep with me until my last day: Here I am videoing my grandmother as she describes her arrival to Auschwitz, the most evil place on Earth.

With my grandparents on my Bat Mitzvah weekend, 1984.

Aftermath

Bubby, Mom and I with newborn Erica (1977). We are topped off by my canopy bed cover, sewn by Bubby, of course.

This is the kind of thing I have been surrounded by my entire life. Relatively recently, I found several encyclopedia-like volumes of books on Bergen-Belsen. Bubby had paper-clipped several comments like this one throughout the book. On one page with a gruesome photo of rows and piles of women's corpses, she had written, "I was walking just next to these corpses. I was there I saw it."

Another favorite. Here I am, with a very pregnant Mom, in front of our first house in Potomac. My dress made by Bubby.

Mom, Bubby and I at my engagement party in 1995.

Aftermath

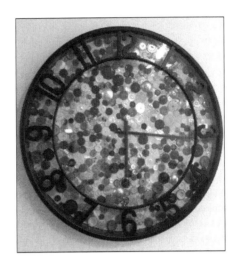

The beautiful and creative clock decorated with Bubby's buttons and hanging in the Space of Mind Schoolhouse in Delray Beach, FL.

My graduation from Penn, 1993.

At the bris, or Jewish circumcision ceremony, of her first great-grandchild, 1998.

Bubby with her granddaughters at Erica's wedding, 2003.

CHAPTER 7

LOVE, MARRIAGE...AND RELIGION

As I was growing up, there were few hard-and-fast rules in my world.

I tended to stay within the lines and do as I was told and expected, so there wasn't much need for laying down the law. I never had a curfew. Without texting, FaceTime or smartphones, it was possible to evade one's parents in ways not possible these days. But as someone who generally followed rules and was generally asleep before ten o'clock every night (still the case), there just weren't any grand opportunities or desires to do crazy things. I wasn't always in the lines, but I also wasn't one to worry much about from a rule-breaking perspective.

One thing that was, however, as nonnegotiable as it gets in my family concerned dating and down the road, marriage. I simply was not allowed to date someone who wasn't Jewish. On this, there was to be no discussion, no questions, no exceptions. Period. And by "Jewish," the person couldn't be "half-Jewish," or have only one parent who was Jewish, or have a Jewish name without the religion to match. It was my duty to marry someone Jewish and bring Jewish kids into the world. My parents went so far as to tell me that they wouldn't pay for or attend my wedding if I decided to marry someone who was of a different or, heaven forbid, no faith.

This may sound awful to some of you. To me—the "me" I am today—it sounds outdated and misguided, even appalling in some regards. It may also sound familiar to others of you who grew up in the Jewish faith. Our religion, Judaism, was at the heart of my grandparents' "they-did-this-to-us-because-we-were-Jewish" story. The moral of this story was that "we would show them." Through our strength and longevity, we would carry on and make sure this never happened to our people again. There are some great lessons about strength and conviction in this approach. There is, also, so much fear in it. And for good reason, of course. Six million people were killed because—and only because—they were Jewish.

So it makes sense that the idea of marrying within your religion so that your religion doesn't die out is one that is all about fear. Fear that religion won't be the most important thing in someone's life. Fear that your grandkids will be of a different religion or have no religion at all. Fear that all of this could lead to another Holocaust. Fear of what will happen if your religion dies out when its numbers dwindle. To my mind, this approach was all about fear and not at all about what other factors should be considered when dating or marrying. But at the time, this was what I was taught, and I was in no position to understand what about it didn't jive with me or with who I would eventually become.

Religion, to me, was all about "have-tos" and "supposed-tos." I thought something was perhaps wrong with me, that I was following something that didn't actually feel like it was part of my soul or that its soul was part of me. Regardless, I had a very specific responsibility: to marry a Jewish man and to bring Jewish kids into the world. This was never up for discussion, and I knew from the very earliest age what my marching orders were here. And while I never, ever tried to change this rule (this would have been an exercise in futility anyway), I did on one or two occasions do what little I could to work around it. When I was in high school, I met a guy with a very "Jewish-sounding" name whom I knew with certainty was actually not Jewish. I told my parents about him and gave his name (that was always the first question, since the last name usually told them all they needed to know), being careful not to mention anything specifically about his religion. They accepted the name without much question, because, as I said, the name could have "passed" as a Jewish one. I think I dated this guy (or whatever it was called back then) for a few months, until it fizzled out. I never had to outright lie, and no non-Jewish kids were born. Likely, they weren't as naive as I pegged them for, but who knows?

(As a sort-of aside: In Judaism, the lineage is maternal, meaning that if the mother is Jewish, the kids are considered Jewish, but my parents and grandparents—like many others with similar backgrounds—were very "all-or-nothing" around this. While I respected it and still do, it is not something that resonates with who I am now. I have found that this kind of an approach or this opinion of just not caring as much feels threatening to some. I know that some of my Jewish friends and readers do not agree and may even feel upset; however, I hope you will respect my views, as I respect yours.)

‡

Non-Jewish guys with Jewish names aside, I always dated the proverbial "Nice Jewish Guys." Always. I did as I was told, and it served me (mostly) well through high school and then college. It wasn't terribly difficult, as I grew up surrounded by Jews and fully immersed in a Jewish community, even attending a Jewish day school for all my high school years. I went on to Penn, which was rumored to be over one-third Jewish. I had lots of crushes on non-Jewish boys (that's a whole other book), but I knew my marching orders. After college, I continued the same socially in New York City. The second year I lived in the City, I quit my job and went on the Eastern Europe trip. A few weeks after that trip, I went to a party on a whim and met the man who would become my husband. He was Israeli, which was a new kind of "Nice Jewish Guy" for me. I was excited to tell my parents, and especially my mom, as well as Bubby, about him. If the goal was to marry a Jewish man, then, I reasoned, marrying an Israeli was like "extra credit" for a job doubly well-done.

He is more of a non-public person than I, and this is not his story or even "our" story, so I want to be respectful of his privacy. Our marriage, subsequent divorce after fifteen years of being together and the co-parenting/friendship/family relationship that has developed in the years since are all, of course, very much parts of the fabric of my life. I know now that I felt enormous pressure—mostly coming from my-self—to marry young and quickly, and to marry "well," that is, to marry a Jewish man. My mother had married my father when she was twenty-three, and I felt I needed to follow in those footsteps. Nobody ever said that to me or indicated that I "had" to get married by a certain point, but I felt that sands-through-the-hourglass urgency of time running short. Perhaps I always wanted to be "the first" for everything (I usually was), or I felt that time was running out (not sure why), but I expected to marry young, and marry young I did. In fact, my two children followed somewhat quickly, and I was all married and mothered-up times two by the age of twenty-eight.

‡

When I became a parent and even before, when I was just thinking about becoming a parent, I knew that the *"Thou shalt marry another Jew"* commandment was not one I would impose on my own kids. I'm not really interested in any "have-tos" unless they are at the level of something like the Golden Rule. The thought of having grandkids who are not Jewish does not consume me. I'm surprised, actually, at how little I care, since this was a dealbreaker in my own childhood. I've learned that for me, being a good person and having the kind of positive impact I hope to have on the world (and that I'm still working on, sometimes less successfully than other times) is not in any way connected to religion, religious affiliation or religious upbringing. I can be a good person, a kind person and yes, a spiritual person, without the inclusion of organized religion. I don't know how someone like my grandmother would have viewed this approach to life, but I am certain she would have wanted me to put kindness and compassion at the top of my list of what truly matters, so I think we're good there.

Today, I am happily part of a long-term, committed relationship with a man who is not Jewish and who, like me, does not actively follow the religion with which he grew up. While I feel profoundly connected to the Jewish roots and traditions that I feel came to me directly from my mother and my grandmother, I do not, by the same token, feel any connection—nor have I ever—to many, if not most, of the practices around Judaism, including prayers, synagogues or hard-and-fast rules regarding things like food or electricity or the roles of men versus women. My kids have been armed with enough insight to make their own informed decisions about how they will go on to live their lives and about what role, if any, religion will play for them.

Aftermath

Accepting and owning all of this took some time and not an insignificant amount of guilt on my part. But today, I am proud of who I am and of how I got here. I'm grateful for all of it and will continue to work hard to become a better person every day.

CHAPTER 8

HOARDING, OCD AND STUFF

Stuff was our connection to the past. It was, we believed, how we remembered. Without it, would we forget? Not likely. But like so many people with so many things, no one could let go. No one had the strength (or, let's face it, even the desire) to start deciding what to let go. And what's more, letting go of the thing that defined so much of who we were sounded weird, scary.

Tossing that which defined you, even if you wanted to grow and perhaps move on from it, was not a possibility in the survivor family. *"You don't throw out food! What if you will need this someday? You can never have too many boxes of this or bottles of that...."*

When Bubby died, I found approximately sixteen large bottles of tonic water, eight jumbo bottles of cranberry juice, twenty-two Kleenex boxes, two eight-packs of paper towels (the big, thick rolls, not the cheap ones I buy) and over twenty bottles of Senekot, an over-the-counter laxative. All of this was "just in case" or "if."

When I was growing up, our house in Potomac, Maryland, was quite large. There was plenty of room for all the stuff we "had to have." In addition to the regular issues of *Newsweek* or *The Economist* (for Dad) or *People* (for Mom), we had enough for a small library annex of Holocaust materials. And over the years, it continued to grow and grow. In the early '90s, Mom asked Dad to donate a large sum of money so an organization representing the survivors of the Lodz Ghetto could compile and publish the names of every person who had lived (and died) in the ghetto. They traveled to Israel for a big ceremony celebrating the completion of this project and honoring them as its benefactors. Following these events, they were, of course, given multiple volumes of the book to bring home and those, too, became part of our permanent collection.

When Mom died, I began to think more and more practically about what would happen to all the Lodz Ghetto books and the many hundreds like them. Dad didn't seem to want to take them with him to his new life and home with the woman who would eventually become his wife. Erica still wasn't settled; she was in college when Mom died and on a temporary year or two in Chicago when Bubby moved to Florida. The idea that the responsibility for all of this stuff—and it was far more than books—would fall on me began to both overwhelm and consume me. Packing up Bubby in Maryland in 2003 was hard enough; unpacking her a few weeks later (now 2004) in Florida was even harder. I already had a house full of stuff I "had" to keep. And living in South Florida, I didn't even have a basement! My life was still surrounded by Holocaust "stuff," and I didn't like it one bit.

The weight of the stuff began to affect me in other areas of my life. When I left for college and later, New York City and then moved to Florida, I felt I'd made a break (not so clean, but a break nonetheless) with my legacy of stuff. Not unlike the child of a hoarder, I felt I had broken a cycle and could now make my own new way, without the stuff weighing me down. What I didn't count on was Mom dying, Bubby packing up and moving here and then dying too. I felt so much responsibility and quite alone in that responsibility. It was only once I got divorced in 2009 and started shedding so much of my past that I began to toss the stuff that had been shaping and following me for decades. I wondered how Bubby, had she been alive, would feel about my throwing so much away. She wouldn't have wanted it, for sure. She would have told me why it was so important to keep all of it. But then I also know that above all else, she wanted me happy. My happiness was what made her happy. And I knew I could not be happy and whole until I started letting go of this past that no one before me could let go of.

‡

It wasn't easy. All of my fears borne out in my "Holocaust Dream" and Bubby losing her beloved butterflies were coming to be. I had to make choices—what stays and what goes. What will remain part of me, and what will I make a break with. To someone who grew up in an environment in which the relationship with the past and with the stuff of the past was more healthy or "normal," this may seem easy to do or even silly. But when you grow up with the past as another living, breathing member of your family, and then you become the only living family member with the ability to house and keep and maintain this stuff, you find yourself having to face many fears and demons you knew would come home to roost someday. I just wasn't really ready for someday. I knew that to break the cycle Mom's friend, Sandy, had talked about twenty years earlier in the mall food court, I had to do things differently. I had to make new decisions and forge ahead based on my own intuition and decisions, not using what I'd been taught or told. It was new and scary and miles from my comfort zone.

I started where I could. I emptied all the '70s-era photo albums and began to divide them by what would be scanned and kept digitally and what would be thrown away. The idea of throwing away the photos of a woman whose entire, post-Holocaust life revolved around making new memories to replace those she had no photos of was upsetting to me. But to keep decades-old photos of people I didn't even know (nor would ever know) seemed unnecessary, as well. And painful, too. Next, there were the books. Including the set commissioned by Dad that took years to complete and came with all sorts of pomp and circumstance with a ceremony in Israel. I knew that books like these belonged in a museum. I emailed and called all the local museums and collections I could find. It wasn't easy to find one that actually wanted donations of books, which, when you think about it, is strange, since their missions are all about keeping this history alive and making sure as many people as possible are exposed to the stories and the works and the resources. Finally, I found a wonderful education center in Hollywood, Florida, that wanted whatever I was willing to donate to them. One day, I drove down there with two or three massive, rolling suitcases, the ones that come as a nifty set you buy but are too big to actually use on a vacation. The suitcases were packed to the gills with heavy books about Lodz and Hitler and ghettos and liberation. The literature of my childhood was being donated. I was relieved and apprehensive at the same time.

The books and the photos made up much of the bulk, both physical and emotional, of the stuff. Interestingly, the clothing held less of an emotional attachment on me, even though for many who lose loved ones, it is the clothing that is hardest to let go of. Fairly soon after Bubby's death, I put all of her clothing into jumbo garbage bags and gave all of it to Tracey, the loving Jamaican woman who took care of Bubby in her final months and who was the only other person with me in the moments after Bubby died. I felt very good about that donation, as Tracey had given so much of herself to Bubby and seemed to love Bubby's taste in clothing and décor. She also mentioned she'd be donating much of it to members of her church, so I was happy it would all be appreciated and enjoyed. I kept a few pieces I wanted for myself, although over the years, I have divested myself of those as well.

‡

Letting go of stuff is like a muscle you need to use and flex, often and consistently. The more you do, I have found, the easier it gets. More than once, I have been accused by my kids of throwing too much away too soon. And they are right about that. I do get overzealous in my tossing at times, likely overcompensating for the lack of tossing I learned growing up. I exhibit this behavior even in my digital life. I am an "over-deleter" of emails, for instance, never allowing them to sit and fester too long in my Inbox. Every year around the December holidays, I go through all of my old documents and emails, culling and trashing where I can.

I have become obsessed with not leaving a mountain of stuff—in all its forms—for my kids or loved ones when I am gone. I don't want anyone to have to hang on to my stuff out of guilt or a sense of duty. If they don't love it or don't need it, I want them to toss it. When I watched all the currently popular shows about hoarders, I felt more than pity or pain for these people and their families. I felt, at a visceral level, a kind of kinship with them, an understanding of sorts. Thankfully, I do not come from a hoarding family, not in the sense or the volume of the people on these shows. But what I did see is that each and every one of them had a starting point.

And every time, that starting point was a massive trauma—a spouse leaving, a death in the family, an empty nest, a loss of a job. These people started out in the same position as all of us. They weren't born as hoarders. Something happened, and it all clicked in a tragic, perfect-storm sort of way. Initially, I was fascinated by the people and the stuff on these shows. I felt a little superior, as if that would never happen to me, and if it happened to someone I loved, then I would know exactly how to fix things. Now, I feel sadness and compassion, so much so that I simply cannot watch those programs anymore.

‡

Another kind of "stuff" that Bubby had was related to her sewing. Bubby had been a highly skilled seamstress all of her adult life. In the ghetto, one of her jobs had been working at a sewing machine, likely doing work for the Nazis who were running the place. It was a coveted job, one that required efficiency and very specific abilities. After she moved to America, Bubby worked professionally as a seamstress, including for the high-end, women's clothing boutique, Lillie Rubin. Her sewing prowess was impressive always, even astounding at times. There was hardly any object and certainly not any item of clothing under Bubby's domain that was not touched by her sewing machine and that had not been altered or beautified in some way. Bubby rarely, if ever, wore clothing straight from the store "as is." She would first customize it, adding her own buttons (often taking off the buttons it came with), additional fabrics, cuffs or a collar. She'd "bedazzle" the boring and build on the interesting. Even a simple house-dress became a one-of-a-kind creation with new buttons and a funky collar.

Once while on a trip to Israel as a counselor for college kids, I was visiting Yad Vashem, the Holocaust museum in Jerusalem. At the time, there happened to be a special exhibit on the Lodz Ghetto (perhaps it had been fifty years since its inception or liberation). I walked into one of the rooms housing the exhibit and looked up at a TV screen showing a video on a loop. The video was made up of black-and-white pictures of daily-life-type scenes in the ghetto. People eating, working, living. I was only half-watching when a picture of a woman at a sewing machine came up on the screen. Bubby! It was Bubby in the video! She was hard at work, deep in con-centration over an item of clothing she had in the machine. She was young, probably mid-to-late-twenties. I stayed in the room until the picture came back and played over again a few times. I didn't know whether to laugh or cry. Laugh at the sheer coincidence or cry at what it reminded me of. No matter how well I knew the stories—all of them—there were times over the years and even today, that the enormity of what really was hits me, and I'm stunned. The young woman at the sewing machine in this video was not only my grand-mother, which in and of itself was mind-blowing enough, but she was a woman being held prisoner, with her entire family and tens of thousands of others, in a place because they were Jewish. The woman in the photo likely didn't yet know what Auschwitz was. She hadn't yet seen her mother be sent in the direction of the gas chamber. Her head hadn't been shaved yet. She was being held prisoner, but this wasn't even the worst part of the story yet. I'd known the story for all of my life; nevertheless, its reality could and still does still stun.

Sewing materials of every imaginable kind were a big part of Bubby's stuff. Buttons, scraps of fabric, pins and needles, thimbles, knitting needles, sequins, ribbons, parts of clothing that she cut off and replaced but didn't discard and so much more. Five decades of the tools of her craft had been left behind to be gone through or tossed altogether. For me, this may have been the hardest as far as determining what would happen to what stuff. As much as anything else and more than most of it, it was sewing that defined so much about Bubby. It was also sewing, I believe, that saved her life over and again. Not just during the war, although that was an enormous part of it, but also after, in America, I believe it gave her something productive and creative and loving to do when she was depressed and lonely and haunted. No matter what was going on around her, she had her machine and her creations. She could literally change, make or fix anything with her hands and her machine. And now I was going to throw it all out?

A lifetime of care and attention with some miracles thrown in…and I was going to toss it all? This was the kind of conundrum that kept me up at night during those years when I was overwhelmed and overrun with stuff from my dead grandmother and mother. Finally, I ended up writing a post on Facebook that went something like this:

"Is there anyone who sews out there? I have an enormous amount of buttons, ribbons, fabrics, elastics and much more from a lifetime of sewing. I'd like for all of this to find a good and appreciative home. Let me know if you or anyone you know would like all of it!"

My friend, Ali, who runs a small and enterprising alternative high school where kids are doing amazing things, answered the call and said that she'd love to take it all to use for crafts and other projects with her kids. What a wonderful idea I'd not even thought of! I was so happy to have found a home for this stuff and grateful that Bubby's sewing would live on through the creative spirit of these kids. After Ali picked it all up from my garage, I was able to cross it off my "Stuff List" and forget about it.

Then one night a year or two later, I went to Ali's school in the town next to mine. We were going to go out to dinner with another girlfriend and decided to all meet up there. As the other friend and I waited on a couch in the school's small entrance area, I looked up at a large, round clock on the wall. It was colorful and fun, its entire face covered by hundreds of buttons of every size and color. Ali saw me gazing up at the clock and must've realized I'd never seen it before.

"You know those are all of your grandmother's buttons, right?"

I was speechless. No, I hadn't known! What a beautiful and unique clock these kids had made. And now Bubby had a place in this school that is changing lives of teenagers and their families. Seeing that clock and learning how it was created with Bubby's buttons was one of many turning points for me and even more so, a moment where I knew she lived on and not just inside of me, but in places I'd never imagined.

‡

When we packed up Bubby for the first time in Maryland in preparation for her move to Florida, I started to discover the enormity of "stuff" she had in the letters department. She had hundreds, if not more, of letters that had come from people of all ages and from all over the United States, thanking her for her story and blessing her for her survival. Some of them had been audience members at one of her talks. They'd been moved and inspired by her stories of survival. They wanted her to know that she'd touched them deeply. So many of those letters came from young people. Then there were letters from folks who had picked up her identification card at the U.S. Holocaust Memorial Museum in Washington, DC. They wanted her to know that they'd randomly picked the card and that, again, her story had touched them. Once they learned that they could write her and share their experience with her (they'd given their letter to the museum, which in turn had forwarded it, thus keeping the contact information of the survivor to themselves), they had to tell her how her personal story had been an integral part of their already-meaningful visit to the museum. Many of these letter writers were people from parts of the U.S. where there were no Jews and certainly no Holocaust survivors. Some of them had never heard much about the Holocaust; most had never met or learned the story of an eyewitness.

To Bubby, these letters were like gold. She reveled in the experience of being the one to introduce the story of the Holocaust to someone who knew little to nothing about it. And certainly her ego loved being told by strangers that she had touched their lives. She wanted to make sure no one forgot the story, and she was happy to be the person who made certain that they did no such thing. In some ways, Bubby fancied herself an ambassador of sorts, talking to people in the way they understood about things they could not possibly relate to or understand but that touched them deeply. No matter what your age or religion or gender, no matter where you lived or what you'd seen and experienced, there was no other story like this story. And to have a woman who looked like she could be anyone's grandmother tell it so eloquently and clearly, and with such detail…well, there was never a person whose soul was not touched in some way.

Today, I have whittled my stash of "Bubby Stuff" down to one large, clear, plastic bin. I don't think I can go less than that, and I won't try. There are treasures in there that I still don't even have the words for, and some likely belong in a museum, at the very least.

CHAPTER 9

BUBBY IN FLORIDA:
TANK TOPS AND ANKLE BRACELETS

So many of those—they were thrown in the grave still being warm, being alive. I can say it with a full heart—I saw it with my own eyes!

As this was going on, I started having pains in my stomach, vomiting, dizziness; I couldn't stand on my feet anymore, which meant that I was stricken with the disease. I went to the hole that was dug by the Nazis because they were still building new barracks for the upcoming transports of people. I put myself in there, wanting and waiting to die.

My friends, the girls, noticed it and came and pulled me out of there by force because I couldn't and wouldn't get up. I also was running a high temperature. The girls succeeded and managed to pull me out of there; four of them.

It was April 14, 1945.

The next day, April the 15th, we were liberated by the British armed forces. I still was very ill and wouldn't believe it. I believed that the Nazis are pulling another trick on us. But I heard an announcement on the microphones in Yiddish and English, and they said, "Kinder sie sind frei!" which means, "Children, you are free."

I believed it then. I could stay here in front of you for years and tell you facts after facts after facts, and I don't think I've told all of it yet!

‡

In the years following Mom's death, Bubby blossomed in new ways. Instead of shrinking into her "sunrise years" as someone who was aging and alone for the first time ever might do, she not only made the best of what she had, but she went out and created a new and relatively exciting life for herself in many ways.

She was unencumbered. For the first time since she was a young girl, she had no one to take care of—not her parents or her siblings, not her husband and not her daughter. No one was relying on her emotionally or in any other way. Financially, she was able to live on Social Security, and her pension and reparation payments from the German government. Her condo was paid for (courtesy of my dad). She lived comfortably and easily, perhaps for the first time ever. She had her hair and nails done religiously. She was always, always, always dressed to the nines. Beautiful suits in bright colors; matching, no-shrinking-violets-allowed hats; coordinating purses; jewelry; face makeup—all on point. She looked fabulous. She was comfortable in her home and in her skin, too.

She became active in her synagogue. It became her primary social outlet. Other families began to "adopt" her as their very own Bubby. Couples who could be her children invited her over for Shabbat dinners, holiday celebrations, birthdays and other family gatherings. She presided over two and sometimes three generations of families, each week in a different home.

"Alkele, they are fighting over me. Sometimes I say yes to two different people, and then I don't know what to do," she would tell me. *"They have to reserve me weeks in advance, and I don't want to say no."* I always told her that she had to learn to say no right away if she knew at the time of the invitation that it wouldn't be possible for her to be in two places at once. She laughed me off in a way that told me this wasn't going to happen. I think she enjoyed seeing what happened when the demand exceeded the supply.

And it was wonderful to watch the "struggles" she endured from all the love and attention of these wonderful families, all of whom welcomed her into their homes as if she were one of their own. They gave her the uncomplicated and unconditional honor and respect she'd likely never before experienced as a recipient. These wonderful people, and I am thinking of at least six or seven families right off the top of my head, showered her with affection. And why not? This was a woman who had earned the love, the comfort, the adulation she was receiving. They gave her a great deal of respect and attention, and she basked in it. It was truly a glorious time for her. I rested easily knowing that she was self-sufficient still, on a day-to-day basis, and that she was more than taken care of in the love and attention department.

When I think of these people and those times today, I realize how fortunate she was to have them and they were to have her. I didn't know them nearly as well as she did, and I rarely see or talk to any of them (they are all in the DC area; I live in Florida), but I think of them as my own family. These people were, literally, lifesavers. I feel thankful to them for all that they gave her in those years, and I feel good knowing she gave them so much in return. Many of them had lost their own elderly parents, or they lived far away. I know at least some had complications with their own blood relatives. They were empty nesters in some cases, new parents in others. They had so much to give her, so much of what truly mattered and what she needed—time, attention, kindness, love. It was a lovely match to see and remains equally lovely to think about after all this time.

As I have shared, following Bubby's death and my subsequent divorce a year or two later, I stopped observing whatever was left in me of organized religion. But when I think of those kind and openhearted people, I see all the best and beautiful reasons that people love their religions: community, tradition, support. They had her back, and they gave her as much as she gave them—probably even more.

Those were good years for Bubby. In some ways, they were her best. She was still speaking in the DC area, and still receiving letters of support and recognition from people of all ages from throughout the U.S.

Things shifted a bit around 2003, however. Five years after Mom died, Bubby experienced one of every elderly person's (and their family's) worst fears: a damaging fall. I never quite got the full story, but she somehow fell in an elevator, thinking that there was a bar along the wall to lean on when in fact, there was not. The force of the fall onto her bottom was so hard and impactful that it broke at least one vertebra and maybe more. It was my understanding at the time, that there is no actual fix for such a break. In a young person, it is a tough injury; in an elderly person, it could be potentially devastating. At this point in time, Bubby was anywhere from her mid-eighties to even ninety-something (it's unclear as to her exact age, as we have already discussed in great detail) and for many of her age, it would not have been surprising for such a break to be the beginning of the end. But while it slowed her down (way down) and changed things, it did not stop her.

Following the injury, Bubby needed more help. Standing up for a long time, as did walking a lot, became issues. She was able to do both, but not as freely and without limits as before. For the first time, she had physical limitations and they affected her psyche, as well.

My sister and I decided that more needed to be done to help Bubby live easier and without worrying that she'd fall again or be alone or be incapacitated in some way. My sister was in Chicago, where her husband was in graduate school, and she was also pregnant. And while living in Chicago was temporary, she didn't know where they'd end up more permanently. I, on the other hand, was more settled down. I lived in a house I owned, and while I had two little kids, they weren't babies, and there were no more babies on the way. The challenge was that I didn't live in Maryland, nor did I have plans to move back there.

Finally we came up with a plan. We (my then-husband and I, with the help of my sister) would come around Christmas of 2003 to help Bubby empty the apartment in Bethesda, where she'd lived since the early '80s. Movers would take the most important furniture and keepsakes down to Florida, and she would follow a week or two later. My dad, with great generosity toward his former mother-in-law, had agreed to buy her a small condo in a "55+" community just a few miles from my home. With the modest income she received from the Germans plus her Social Security, there would be a small amount of money left over to pay someone to help her out a few hours per day. With me to supplement in the caregiving department, we'd do our best to make this work. I was working full-time and had my own domestic responsibilities, so full-time caregiving was not an option for me, and thankfully she did not need it at that time.

Packing up that apartment was a bear. The apartment contained a lifetime of letters, photos, artifacts, memories and reminders. As always, the common link was the Holocaust. The books, the correspondence, the souvenirs—all of it was connected to Bubby being a survivor. Who could throw away any of these things? They were not just part of her history; they were part of everyone's history. We owed it to "them" (whomever they were or are) to keep these things, right? Even though Bubby was moving to a small condo with very little storage capabilities, we needed to find a way to continue to house history. Bubby was both a neat freak and someone who kept a lot—A LOT—of stuff.

Bubby moved into her new home in January of 2004. Right away, she informed me she did not want to explore the Century Village social life because she did not want to be friends with "old people." She did show some interest in the Holocaust Survivors Club, so I made sure to find out when and where the club met. (I shudder to think of how thin this group's membership is today—if, in fact, it even still exists.) While the community, like a little city unto itself, provided bus service from each group of buildings to the clubhouse, which was the center of social life, Bubby also refused to ride the bus "with the old people." (Keep in mind, she was likely in her early nineties at this point.)

I don't remember her ever taking public transportation anywhere, and I believe this block against getting on a public bus tied into her need to be in control, to be the driver, literally and figuratively. I believe she also had anxiety around using transportation with many people, all strangers, and being driven somewhere by a stranger. The experience of being stuffed into the cattle cars from the Lodz Ghetto to Auschwitz haunted her life until her last day, and I believe she was reminded of some element of that experience when she thought about getting on a bus in Century Village. Of course, there was no connection to the average person, but I understood how she thought, and she was not the average person. By this point in my life, I didn't ask questions or wonder things like, "*How on earth is there a connection between the Century Village bus in Boca Raton, Florida, and the trains to and from hell in Poland?*" At some point, we stop questioning and start understanding, even if the "average" person wouldn't see the same thing. Also, the older I got, the more I understood in a very real way.

Since I lived so close by, it was easy enough for me to drive her to and from the survivors' meeting or any other social events she wanted to attend. As it turned out, however, she never made any effort to become part of the social life in her new surroundings. She didn't like the old people. She didn't want to ride the bus. She'd come from a community that knew and respected her, that revered and celebrated her. These weren't her people. Here, she wasn't known. She wasn't somebody. She was another old person. She was thrilled to be living near me and my family, and that she wasn't alone with her back injury anymore. But a lot of her identity had been left back in Maryland, and I imagine that must have been tough.

One day that I was feeling particularly worried about Bubby, I decided to drive over before I had to pick up the kids from school. I mentally rehearsed what I'd say to her, how she had to make an effort to adapt to her new surroundings, that this was now her home, to give people and activities a chance and so on. I was still going over all of my talking points in my head when she answered the door. I stared at her and was speechless. Everything I'd planned to say and repeated in my head disappeared. My grandmother was always a woman who dressed modestly and somewhat formally every day of her life since I'd known her. She was so fashionable and had true style, but always a long skirt or dress of some sort and rarely bare legs, unless she was home in a housedress. And now she was standing before me in the South Florida humidity in a hot-pink, ribbed tank top; white cotton capris to her mid-calf and a thick gold anklet with matching necklace to complete the look.

I think the anklet was probably my favorite part.

I stared, my mouth so wide open that my jaw likely almost hit the floor.

"Bubby, what are you wearing?"

"You like it, Alkele? It's so hot here, I had to buy some new clothes. Come look what else I got."

She led me inside into the apartment, down a narrow hallway and back into her spare bedroom. She opened a drawer and inside were three, neatly stacked rows of plastic-wrapped packages containing the same ribbed tank top in every imaginable color and then some.

Bubby was nothing if not adaptable. She quickly picked up the ways of wherever she was, and she not only did so quickly, but she thrived in the process. Even at her advanced age, she was still so self-aware and able to act on it quickly. She didn't want to be friends with the "old people" in Century Village. So instead she went out and found friends a couple of decades younger. They adored her, and she adored being adored.

For the first time in her life, she was living for herself and only herself. She was being taken care of, and she was enjoying that. Her sadness, her trauma—it was behind her. A part of her, sure, but in the past. She was determined to enjoy her remaining time, and if that meant avoiding "old people" and wearing tank tops in every color of the rainbow, then so be it.

Epilogue:
TRAUMA: INHERITED, INCORPORATED, HEALED

THIS STUDY SUGGESTS THAT DESPITE THE FACT THAT THE Holocaust occurred over 60 years ago, it continues to exist, and in some cases thrive, both consciously and unconsciously, in the lives of third generation members. Moreover, a corollary intent of the study was to suggest that a traumatic event, especially one which occurs to a particular ethnic group, can impact individuals of future generations, irrespective of their race or religion.

The individuals who participated in this study clearly indicated that they were, to varying degrees, impacted by the Holocaust. Despite the fact that many of the participants were not overtly symptomatic or even likely to fall under the heading of "intergenerational trauma," they were capable of thinking about the Holocaust, making meaning of their experiences, and under-

standing the unique ways in which the Holocaust affected their behaviors, relationships, and worldviews.

Moreover, while each individual's lived experience was indeed unique, there were certain common themes which emerged from the study. They included the perceived impact of the Holocaust on some of the participants' sense of selves, fantasies and dreams, emphases on remembering, relationships to their respective COS [Child of Survivor] parents and HS [Holocaust Survivor] grandparents, relationships to Germany, German people and German things, and finally, familial home environments.

~ Joshua Micah Simmons in his 2008 doctoral dissertation *The Unconscious Never Forgets: A Qualitative Exploratory Study of Jewish Grandchildren of Survivors of the Nazi Holocaust* **(used with permission)**

Aftermath

NEVER AGAIN! ONE OF THE HALLMARKS OF A HOLOCAUST survivor family is the idea of remembrance; the guiding principle that such a history could be forgotten—and thus could potentially happen again—is ingrained into 3Gs as something akin to the greatest tragedy one could imagine. Remembrance is a "hot button" issue in the Jewish community today, as it was in the '70s and '80s, when the survivors began coming out of the closet and telling their stories to the public and to their young grandchildren. Throughout my twenties and thirties, I struggled with this legacy that was at once a source of enormous pride, a heavy responsibility and an emotional burden.

For me, and I know for other 3Gs, the grandparent/ grandchild relationship—and my relationship with Bubby, in particular—was one of the cornerstones of my identity and a true guidepost as far as how I viewed myself and my family in relation to the world.

Your ancestors' lousy childhoods or excellent adventures might change your personality, bequeathing anxiety or resilience by altering the epigenetic expressions of genes in the brain.

Like silt deposited on the cogs of a finely tuned machine after the seawater of a tsunami recedes, our experiences, and those of our forebears, are never gone, even if they have been forgotten. They become a part of us, a molecular residue holding fast to our genetic scaffolding. The DNA remains the same, but psychological and behavioral tendencies are inherited. You might have inher-

ited not just your grandmother's knobby knees, but also her pre-disposition toward depression caused by the neglect she suffered as a newborn.

~ **"Grandma's Experiences Leave a Mark on Your Genes"** (*Discover Magazine* May 2013)

‡

Aftermath

Do a Google search using terms like "inherited trauma" and "Holocaust," and you are sure to find quite a debate as to whether this is a "thing." Both "sides" are adamant that theirs is the correct one, that they have the facts and research to back up their claims. Truth be told, I don't much care about who is saying what, and whose research is better or "more" right. I know what my experience has been. I know firsthand what growing up immersed and enmeshed in the story of the Holocaust has done to my personality, to my nature, to my way of being, doing and seeing both within myself and within the greater world. (By the way, if my future grandchildren or great-grandchildren are reading this, I'm sorry for the overreacting-to-stress gene I've most certainly passed on. But we do have that smart gene thing going on, am I right?)

"…descendants of people who survived the Holocaust have different stress hormone profiles than their peers, perhaps predisposing them to anxiety disorders."

~ "An Investigation of Potential Holocaust-Related Secondary Trauma in the Third Generation" (*Scientific American* March 1, 2015)

‡

I COULD WRITE MY OWN PHD THESIS ON THE LESSONS I learned, lived, breathed, absorbed and at times, devoured and/or rejected as the granddaughter of Paula Dash and the daughter of Lily Blankstein. I saw in them who I was, and where I came from. I also saw who I was not, and where I preferred not to go. I saw what I wanted, and what I rejected. I've embraced, then rejected and then embraced it all again so many times that my arms are just...tired.

Bubby took the very worst that life has to offer and created a life that was empowering and inspiring to her and to everyone who came into contact with her. Did she have special powers or a certain kind of training that gave her the strength she needed to live in this way? I don't think so. She was a Jewish woman from a city in Poland, perhaps on the worldly and sophisticated side by the standards of the day and place, but not someone who would have left her life to pursue anything beyond what it could offer her. Had it not been for the war and all the disruption that came with it, she would've stayed in Poland with her childhood sweetheart-husband, had kids and lived in that era's version of happily ever after.

Of course, none of that was to be. Everything changed and nothing lasted. She started over with nothing, really less than nothing, in a country that wasn't hers. I know I would have crumbled under the pressure; the devastation of a life so overwhelmingly traumatized and born again into uncertainty would have done me in. More than just adapt, she became one of the most patriotic, dedicated, outspoken Americans I've ever known.

Oh, she battled her demons, to be sure. She endured nightmares throughout her life—first, she lived them and then, for the rest of time, she recalled them. I know many of them involved the night she arrived at Auschwitz after a horrendous and terrifying three days in the cattle car, only to have her mother ripped from her and sent to the gas chamber, never to be seen alive again. She still saw in her mind's eye the hundreds of corpses, piled high in a pit that seemed to be growing by the minute. Maybe she wondered what would have happened if she had jumped in as she tried to before her friends saved her. Regardless, she lived a very long, full and utterly remarkable life, as sharp and in control as ever until her death at the end of 2007, at the age of anywhere up to ninety-five.

And yet all of that, which to me was miraculous and heroic, was to Mom burdensome and heavy. Her entire life was one of longing. She would never have chosen that history for herself. She wanted to come from another family, another time, another place. She wanted to be someone different. She so wanted detachment, yet she spent her entire life wholly and in many ways detrimentally attached to the very past she so resented. I once had a psychic tell me that she knew I couldn't depend on my mom, that her energy wasn't mature enough to give to her family and that her soul wasn't ever coming back.

The Holocaust is hardly the only life crisis that can shape behavior and genes. Survivors of Afghanistan, Iraq or Darfur — or even those who grew up in unstable or abusive homes — can exhibit similar changes. But Holocaust survivors remain one of the best study groups available because their trauma was so great, their population is so well known, and so many of them have gone on to produce children, grandchildren and even great-grandchildren.

~ **"Genetic Scars of the Holocaust: Children Suffer Too"** (*TIME* **Magazine Sept 09 2010**)

‡

Aftermath

Today, I am nearing the end of my own first stage of parenting. My kids—now young adults—are turning seventeen and nineteen this year. When they were younger, as I began to come to terms with my own upbringing, I vowed to make theirs different. At the same time, I was still examining, wrestling with, finally coming to truly understand, my own "stuff." In my late thirties, much of this started to "come back up," and I knew I had to face it once and for all. That included (but was certainly not limited to) ending my marriage, examining and healing food issues that had plagued me for decades and realizing that my perfectionist ways were neither sustainable nor healthy. Along the way, I have since found love—with my loving partner; with and from my kids, who have become incredible humans in their own right; with my former husband, who is now a treasured part of the group I consider my true family and most importantly within myself, for myself.

More than anything, I wanted to feel more whole and healed than broken. I knew it wouldn't be easy, but I did know it was possible. I was determined to truly break the cycle in a way that my mom had not been able to do. To this day, while my kids know that Bubby (who was present for the first eight to ten years of their lives) and Zeidy (whom they never knew) survived the Holocaust, they don't know all the finer, minute details that, in so many ways, made up the very essence of my own childhood. While they know that Grandma Lily died by suicide four months after my son was born, and that it is her name represented by my daughter's middle name, they don't know all the details, reasons, explanations and stories. There were never secrets, and I have never held back when asked about anything, but there was also never a burning need to dump all that had been dumped on me right onto the next generation.

Some might think that their not knowing it all is sad, or maybe that it represents somewhat of a missed opportunity. Or, perhaps, that I am keeping the future world from knowing what we have already determined to be something to "never forget." I would respectfully disagree. To me, this divergence from the way it's always been is the result of a very conscious decision that is and was, in fact, a true act of compassion. It's my way of bringing healing not just to myself, but even more importantly, to my kids. Filling my kids' childhood with stories of the Holocaust did not represent to me the kind of parent I wanted to be. The fine line where memory ends and burden begins is likely different for different people. I do not in any way see my deliberate decision to not go this route as a rejection of where and what I came from; if anything, it is the ultimate acceptance. Either way, I am proud of the beautiful, young adults I have raised, and I am—always—proud of the history that produced me. Without it, I would not be here. I know this now and always will.

Remember the story of the butterflies? It's part of who I am and who I have become. Their beauty is in my cells; it is part of my soul. At the same time, their impermanence, the sadness they represent and the feeling of impending doom that never quite leaves my consciousness are all, as well, part of every fiber of my being. Nothing—humans included—is perfect and without blemish. My lessons—about patience, perfectionism, truth and so much more—are blessings and lifelong companions, to be learned and learned again. I now know that I can be healed and whole, while still being imperfect. For this realization and for at least a million more, I bow in gratitude to those who came before me: my mom, Bubby, Zeidy and all of my family, and the millions of others who never had the chance to live their full lives, who never had the luxury to fully express themselves. I see you, and I thank you.

Allison Nazarian
Boca Raton, FL
July 2016

*A*PPENDIX:

THE LESSONS

A t one point, when the idea of this book seemed too big and daunting, I thought, "Maybe I will instead write a light book on the fun but key lessons I learned from Bubby." While that would've been a lovely little book, I know now (as I am sure I also knew then) that that wasn't the book I was meant to write.

However, I didn't want to let these gems of "Bubby Lessons" go without acknowledging them:

You never know when you'll need an extra forty-two rolls of toilet paper.

If the story doesn't fit, change the story.

Don't be ashamed to be the best.

Aftermath

Never buy generic.

If you think you're right, then you're right.

If it's on the TV news, then it's the truth.

The children of your children can do no wrong.

Everyone needs to eat a carb.

Dress to the nines—no matter what the occasion.

Rules are fine—unless they cramp your style.

First impressions are the only impression.

A person who questions Elvis's greatness is not to be trusted.

Age is but a useless number.

Never settle for less than exactly what you want, how you want it.

Maintaining a good marriage takes the planning of a war general.

Always question someone who says they are from Lodz—they are probably from a village outside of Lodz.

ACKNOWLEDGMENTS

There is nothing I love more than a good thank you, and there is no heart fuller than mine right now.

To the first person not related to me who made me feel like this could actually someday be a book and for a lot more all the way back in 1997, I give you, Sam Freedman, author, reporter and teacher extraordinaire, the greatest thanks from the deepest places in my heart and soul.

For writing and editing help, guidance, insight and patience, thank you to Stephanie Gunning, Brooke Warner and Nicholas Garnett.

To the 150+ 3G interviewees who shared with me your time and your story, I salute you and thank you. I give you, in return, my story.

Thank you to family friends who filled in some holes, shared memories and insights and gave me the time of day: Claire Simmons, Joshua Simmons, Mindy Weisel, Carolyn Weisel Miller and Jon Kushner. To my Aunt Gladys who has always been such a dear and loving cheerleader, and has never forgotten anything in her entire life. Thank you to Arie Reich, my brilliant and helpful cousin in Israel. A huge hug and everlasting thank you to Shelly Winchester, a loving, patient and giving cousin who shared so much with me and understands all of this all too well. To Helga Matzko, who helped me early on with some German translations, thank you for your help. To one of the coolest women I've known but never actually met face-to-face, Lori Albrecht Barnett, for all of the transcriptions you took care of over the years. I'm pretty sure you had no idea what you were getting in to early on. To Rick Holland, for the perfect cover design and for getting exactly what I was looking for almost immediately. To Karyn Martin, a fine and meticulous editor, lots of love and Oxford commas to you. Of course, any errors, omissions of confusion of any kind in this book are fully and solely my responsibility and my doing.

To my first readers, a group of brilliant, responsive and giving women who volunteered to read through a semi-mess of a book and gave so generously of their time and feedback: Alissa, Wendy, Stefanie, Reese and Mariana. What generous and wonderful friends and editors you all are! While on the topic of wonderful women, thank you to my OG Squad of tried-and-true friends who offer endless support and laughs, especially this year: Jennifer, Deb, Bonnie, Jill, Tammy and Claire. Thank you to my Mastermind women, new as a group but not new as amazing friends in my life: Michelle, Dawn, Reese, Stefanie, Elizabeth and Peggie. What gifts you each are to me! Another special thank you to my kids' Abba, Asher: You have always supported me telling this story, and you will always be part of my treasured inner circle of family and friends.

To my sister, Erica: We're so different in many ways, but I know that you know what I know, and you know I know the same. (Make sense?) I love you, through thick and thin. To Lily and Evan, what a privilege it is to have a front-seat to watching you two amazing people grow up. I know that Bubby and Grandma Lily are always watching over you. A special added shout-out to you, Lily, and to the wonderful author you are.

To Nick: The unconditional way you love and support me is reminiscent only of one other person in my life, my Bubby. You're my kind, patient, funny and deeply loving rock, and I am so grateful for all that you do.

To Zeidy: I wish we could've had more time together. I know you are resting easy wherever you are, and I hope the vending machines there are great. To Dad: I'd hoped to finish this book in time for you to read it, but that wasn't to be. Your generosity with Bubby and Zeidy will always be remembered by so many people. And it is because of you that books and reading always were—and still are—front and center in my life.

To Mom and Bubby: Without you, there is no book, so it's probably best to get in another thank you here. To this day, when I hear a certain accent in an overheard conversation, I think of you, of us, of what might've been. I am who

Aftermath

I am because of both of you. There is not a day that goes by during which I don't wonder what you'd say about this or that. I can only imagine how much fun we might all have together these days. There will always be a part of me that continues to ask "*What if…?*"

To Daniel and Maya: Do I thank you? Do I ask you to thank me? (Ha.) In many ways, this is your story and the story in your cells. (Don't debate me on the science, Daniel.) It's the story I was born to write, and the one you are now ready to read and, I hope, pass on some day. I started this before you were born and now, like both of you, it is ready to fly. Always remember it's never too late to finish or get started or change course or just start a whole new way. Go with your gut and remember you are always in charge of your own life. I love you both endlessly and wildly, and I thank you for understanding (and sometimes pretending to care) about what I had to do and why I had to do it.

ABOUT THE AUTHOR

A GRADUATE OF THE UNIVERSITY OF PENNSYLVANIA AND
Columbia University's School of Journalism, Allison Nazarian is an award-winning copywriter and the founder of Allison Media Group. A native of the Washington, DC area,
Allison lives with her family in South Florida.

To learn more about this book or to contact Allison for
speaking, interviewing or sharing, visit **The3GBook.com**.

Printed in Great Britain
by Amazon